ASIAN
COOKERY IN COLOUR

ASIAN
COOKERY IN COLOUR

JACKI PASSMORE

SUMMIT BOOKS
Published by Paul Hamlyn Pty Limited
Sydney · Auckland · London · New York

Summit Books
Published by Paul Hamlyn Pty Limited
176 South Creek Road, Dee Why West, NSW, Australia, 2099
First published 1979
©Copyright Paul Hamlyn Pty Limited 1979
Produced in Australia by the Publisher
Printed by Kyodo Shing Loong Printing Industries Pte Ltd
112 Neythal Road, Jurong Town, Singapore 22.

National Library of Australia Cataloguing-in-Publication Data

Passmore, Jacki
    All Asian cookery in colour

    Index
    ISBN 0 7271 0385 7

    1. Cookery . I. Title .
641.59'5

CONTENTS

INTRODUCTION

In recent years, increasing numbers of Westerners have discovered the wide variety of excellent dishes produced in Asia; they've also learned that most of this fascinating food can be easily prepared in a Western kitchen with a minimal amount of special utensils.

The large curved-based pan generally known by its Chinese name, *wok,* is familiar to most Western cooks and is a thoroughly worthwhile investment, for it is used in almost all Asian cooking. A steamer is also useful, though any really large pan that will accommodate food placed on a rack makes an adequate substitute. The traditional charcoal barbecue can be replaced by a gas or electric griller. A powerful blender, food processor or coffee grinder can take the place of the mortar and pestle or granite grinding slab used in Asia, where spices are usually ground just before use.

Asian Cookery in Colour brings you familiar delights from India and China, as well as excitingly different dishes from Indonesia, Thailand, The Philippines, Malaysia and Singapore, and Japan. Chinese stores, specialty food shops and even supermarkets now stock the spices, dried goods and other basic ingredients required. The glossary at the back of this book explains some of the less familiar ingredients and suggests substitutes wherever possible, while techniques are clearly explained in every recipe. The East is no longer inscrutable!

INDIA: To most cooks, Indian food means curry. Although many excellent curries are, of course, prepared in India, curry by no means constitutes the entire Indian cuisine. There are wonderful dry spiced meat and vegetable dishes; poultry and meat roasted in an enclosed pot over a slow fire; a host of different kinds of breads, rice and lentil dishes; superb rich desserts and sweetmeats; and an endless variety of vegetarian dishes that make up the diet of more than half the Indian population.

But to return to curry (which, incidentally, comes from the Tamil word *kari,* meaning 'sauce'). An Indian cook never uses the commercial curry powders known in the West, but blends a mixture of whole dried spices, heats them to bring out the flavour, then grinds them to a powder just before use. *Garam masala,* a mixture of at least six spices, is the nearest thing in India to a curry powder. It is used together with other spices, or is sometimes sprinkled over a finished dish as additional seasoning.

Although beef is never eaten by Hindu Indians, the cow contributes milk which is almost always on the table in one form or another: as rich buttery sweets, creamy sauces, home-made cheeses cooked in spicy curries, and yoghurt. Yoghurt is used to thicken sauces and tenderise meat; it is also combined with salad ingredients or mixed with water and flavoured with salt or sugar to make a delicious drink called *lassi.*

An Indian meal consists of the staple (rice or bread) together with main dishes (meat, poultry, fish, lentils and vegetables) and a variety of accompaniments to add piquancy (freshly made chutneys, pickles, preserves, and fried *poppadum* — a lentil wafer).

INDONESIA: It is not surprising that the food of many areas in Indonesia should be seasoned with spices, for the Moluccan islands in the eastern part of the archipelago were the original 'Spice Islands'. Indonesia is a widespread region encompassing many different people and cultures, and this diversity is reflected in the food.

The cuisines of Sumatra and Java are the best known in the outside world, and are arguably the most delicious. Bali, while the most popular island from the tourist's point of view, does not have a highly developed cuisine, although there are several remarkably good dishes. Sumatran cooks use a greater number of spices and herbs than do other Indonesians, and frequently simmer food in rich coconut-milk sauces given a hint of sourness by the addition of tamarind juice. Javanese cooking tends to be sweeter, using brown palm sugar in many meat and vegetable dishes as well as in desserts and cakes. The influence of the Chinese, who have traded and lived in Indonesia for centuries, is evident in the widespread liking for noodles, beancurd products, and soya sauce — although the Javanese typically add palm sugar to turn the latter into a thick sweet salty liquid.

In most of Indonesia, rice is the staple. It is served together with several dishes containing meat, poultry, fish and vegetables, and enlivened by side dishes of *sambal,* condiments usually based on chillies.

THAILAND: Eating Thai food is a multiple experience: taste buds, eyes and nose are all completely involved with heady aromas, brilliant colours, sour, sweet, pungent and stingingly hot tastes. It seems that nothing is too ordinary, or too exotic, to go into the cooking pot in Thailand. Some dry spices are encountered, but the flavouring is most likely to be provided by ginger, fresh turmeric root, *kha* (a ginger-like root), garlic, shallots, lemon grass, citrus juice and leaves, roots and leaves of the coriander plant, *kapi* (a dried shrimp paste similar to Malaysian *blacan* and Indonesian *trasi*) and *nam pla* (the ubiquitous fish sauce, with a salty flavour somewhat similar to light soya sauce). And then there are the chillies — red and green, long and short. Beware of the tiny innocuous-looking bird's-eye chillies that pack the biggest punch of all!

Fresh coconut milk provides the lovely rich creamy sauce that bathes many Thai dishes; there are also many dishes where the main ingredient is fried in a little oil, then splashed with a small amount of stock or fish sauce. Salads are one of the many delightful aspects of Thai cuisine. Always beautiful to look at, they combine small amounts of meat (generally pork) or seafood with crisp, often tart, vegetables or fruits such as water chestnuts, lotus root, unripe papaya or mango, bamboo shoots and white radish.

Rice (and long-grain Thai rice is among the world's best) is the mainstay of every meal. It is served together with a soup and several main dishes, and followed either by fresh fruit or by one of the many artistic Thai desserts. Rice flour, mung-bean flour, or mashed tubers such as tapioca are combined with coconut milk and palm sugar to make a wonderfully rich and generally fragrant finish to a meal.

Peking Duck (frontispiece), and a selection of Dim Sum.

THE PHILIPPINES: Perhaps more than any other country in Asia, the Philippines reveals its history in its food — the influence of four hundred years of Spanish rule, of even longer Chinese contact, and of twentieth-century America. Where else could you begin the day with 'native' cakes made from rice and coconut milk, eat a bowl of Chinese noodles for lunch, have a late afternoon snack of hamburger and icecream, and finish off with a *paella* for supper?

The food served during fiestas — and there are plenty of these — almost invariably presents the truly Filipino roast suckling pig (Lechon), while other dishes are likely to be Spanish in origin. Although lacking the inventiveness of Chinese cuisine, the rich spicing of India and Indonesia, and the beautiful simplicity of Japanese dishes, Filipino food has plenty of surprises in store. Some of the snack foods, such as Lumpia (a type of fresh spring roll filled with salad) or cakes made with rice flour and coconut milk, are truly excellent, while *adobo* dishes redolent with garlic and black pepper can hold their own anywhere.

MALAYSIA AND SINGAPORE: It is difficult to separate the cooking of Malaysia and neighbouring Singapore, countries sharing so much in the way of history and cultural make-up. Their food benefits from the three major racial groups living side by side: traditional Chinese, Malay and Indian dishes are available everywhere, but that's not all — distinctly local dishes, the result of a mingling of cooking styles, add yet another dimension to the culinary delights of the region.

The majority of the Chinese who migrated to Malaysia and Singapore came from southern China, so the most common types of Chinese food are Cantonese and Hokkien dishes. However, they are invariably served with a side dish of sliced green chillies or a hot red chilli *sambal*, the result of the Chinese living alongside the chilli-loving Malays and Indians.

Malay dishes, especially the coconut-milk curries pungent with a host of spices, often include several herbs and leaves reminiscent of Thai cooking, while *blacan* (dried shrimp paste) and *asam* (sour tamarind juice) are an indispensable part of the local Malay cuisine. All types of Indian food are found in Malaysia and Singapore, the most common being the southern styles of the Madras region and Kerala.

Food reflecting the intermingling of Chinese and Malay culinary traditions is known as 'Nonya' cooking; this is the name given to women who were descendants of Chinese men and Malay women who married in the days when there were almost no Chinese women in the region. And in Malacca, there are still culinary traces of the Portuguese who ruled the city in the sixteenth century.

JAPAN: Despite their proximity to China and Korea, the Japanese have developed a cuisine that is unique in its delicacy of taste and splendid simplicity. Those unfamiliar with Japanese food may dismiss it as being too unusual, yet few who have the patience to experiment are not won over to this excellent cuisine. The Japanese ideal is to bring out the essential flavours of the basic ingredients, not to mask them with strong seasonings and rich heavy sauces. The food is only just cooked, and flavoured in such a subtle fashion that when you eat it, it seems as if you are tasting the genuine flavours of the food for the very first time.

Much Japanese cooking concentrates on seafood, for Japan is an island country, while beancurd, vegetables and pork are also very important. Although top quality beef is produced in Japan, it is prohibitively expensive and eaten infrequently (and then in small quantities). Soya sauce — even the Chinese will recommend Japanese brands — and rice wine (either regular *sake* or the sweetened version called *mirin*) are the main seasonings. Horseradish paste (*wasabi*), certain types of seaweed, and *miso* (a thick paste made from fermented soya beans) are also widely used.

Japanese food is seldom fried, and is more easily digested than most other Asian food. *Dashi,* the basic stock used in many dishes, hints vaguely of the sea with its flavouring of seaweed and dried bonito fish. Another quality that sets Japanese food apart is the emphasis on presentation, for the Japanese believe that the appearance of food is every bit as important as the flavour. Consideration is given even to the type of dish on which the food is served, and the season.

CHINA: Chinese cooking scarcely needs any introduction, for cooks all over the world have long acknowledged it as one of the major cuisines, on a par with that of France. Yet many cooks are familiar only with Cantonese food: they are unaware of the delights of Shanghainese dishes, rich and savoury; of Peking, sophisticated and satisfying; Szechwan, with its fiery flavours; or the distinctive styles of Fukien province and of the earthy Hakka people.

One of the most striking aspects of Chinese cooking is the unique blending of different ingredients, which throws traditional Western concepts out the window. Chinese cuisine combines meats, seafoods and vegetables in infinite variations based on the principles of harmony and contrast. Each dish, and the meal as a whole, will have a balance of taste, texture and colour.

Soya sauce, spring onions, ginger and garlic are the most important seasoning ingredients. Salted black beans, a range of sweet and salty bean pastes, and a mixture of spices called 'five-spice powder' are also frequently used. Rice or noodles are served at every meal, usually with a variety of other dishes that are placed on the table at the one time for all to share. Soup is also served during the meal; only if it is a very special soup, such as sharksfin, it is served at the beginning.

Most Chinese cooking is done in a curved pan called a *wok.* A common technique is stir frying in a small amount of oil over high heat, which quickly seals in the flavour and goodness of the food. The *wok* is also used for deep frying and even for steaming food. The preparation of food prior to cooking is usually more time-consuming than the cooking itself, and because Chinese food should be served immediately after it is cooked, the cook needs to plan in advance.

WEIGHTS & MEASURES

The metric weights and metric fluid measures used throughout this book refer to those of The Standards Association of Australia (AS 1325 1972). A good set of scales, a graduated Australian Standard measuring cup and a set of Australian Standard measuring spoons will be most helpful. These are available at leading hardware and kitchenware stores.
• The Australian Standard measuring cup has a capacity of 250 millilitres (250 ml).
• The Australian Standard tablespoon has a capacity of 20 millilitres (20 ml).
• The Australian Standard teaspoon has a capacity of 5 millilitres (5 ml).

New Zealand, Canadian and American weights and measures are the same except that the Australian Standard measuring tablespoon has a capacity of 20 millilitres (20 ml), whereas the New Zealand, Canadian and American Standard measuring tablespoons have a capacity of 15 millilitres (15 ml).

All spoon measurements given in this book are level spoonfuls.

Weight, volume and liquid measures
In all recipes, imperial equivalents of metric measures are shown in parentheses, e.g. 500 g (1 lb) lean beef. Although the metric yield of cup or weighed measures is approximately 10% greater, the proportions remain the same. For successful cooking use either metric weights and measures *or* imperial weights and measures — do *not* use a mixture of the two.

The following tables are extracted from conversion equivalents adopted by the Cookery Sector Committee of the Metric Conversion Board (Australia).

IMPERIAL			METRIC	
Liquid Measures	Cup Measures		Cup Measures	Liquid Measures
1 fl oz		is replaced by		30 ml
2 fl oz	¼ cup	,,	¼ cup	
	⅓ cup	,,	⅓ cup	
3 fl oz		,,		100 ml
4 fl oz (¼ pint US)	½ cup	,,	½ cup	125 ml
5 fl oz (¼ pint imp.)		,,		150 ml
6 fl oz	¾ cup	,,	¾ cup	185 ml
8 fl oz (½ pint US)	1 cup	,,	1 cup	250 ml
10 fl oz (½ pint imp.)	1¼ cups	,,	1¼ cups	
12 fl oz	1½ cups	,,	1½ cups	
14 fl oz	1¾ cups	,,	1¾ cups	
16 fl oz (1 pint US)	2 cups	,,	2 cups	500 ml
20 fl oz (1 pint imp.)	2½ cups	,,	2½ cups	

Mass (Weight)		Mass (Weight)
½ oz	is replaced by	15 grams (g)
1 oz	,,	30 g
2 oz	,,	60 g
3 oz	,,	90 g
4 oz (¼ lb)	,,	125 g
6 oz	,,	185 g
8 oz (½ lb)	,,	250 g
12 oz (¾ lb)	,,	375 g
16 oz (1 lb)	,,	500 g (0.5 kg)
24 oz (1½ lb)	,,	750 g
32 oz (2 lb)	,,	1000 g (1 kg)
3 lb	,,	1500 g (1.5 kg)
4 lb	,,	2000 g (2 kg)

INDIA

MULLIGATAWNY SOUP

250 g (½ lb) chicken
5 cups chicken stock
1 large onion
3 cloves garlic
2 fresh red chillies, thinly sliced
2 tablespoons *ghee*
1 tablespoon coriander, ground
¼ teaspoon fenugreek, crushed
1 teaspoon cummin, ground
1 teaspoon turmeric powder
1 bay leaf
2.5 cm (1 inch) stick cinnamon
2 black cardamoms
2 cloves
salt
pepper
¾ cup thick coconut milk

Place chicken and stock in a large saucepan with sliced onion. Bring to the boil and simmer for 30 minutes. Mash garlic and chillies and fry in *ghee* for 2 minutes. Add all remaining spices and fry for 2 minutes. Add to the pot and continue cooking until chicken is tender.

Lift out chicken and cut into small dice. Return to the soup. Season to taste and stir in thick coconut milk. Heat through.

FRIED MEAT SNACKS

MEAT SAMOOSA

frozen spring roll wrappers
250 g (½ lb) minced beef or mutton
¼ cup water
1 clove garlic, minced
1 small onion, minced
1 cm (½ inch) piece fresh ginger, minced
2 teaspoons *garam masala*
1 teaspoon chilli powder
1 teaspoon black mustard seeds
½ teaspoon turmeric powder
salt
black pepper
1 heaped tablespoon chopped fresh coriander leaves
2 tablespoons frozen peas (optional)
2 teaspoons lemon juice
2 tablespoons *ghee*
oil for deep frying

Thaw wrappers and wrap in a damp cloth until needed. Cook minced meat in water until the liquid has completely dried up. Fry minced garlic and onion in *ghee* for 3 minutes. Add ginger, meat and *garam masala* and fry for a further 3 minutes. Add remaining ingredients and heat through thoroughly. Leave to cool.

Cut spring roll wrappers into 4 cm (1½ inch) strips and fold one end over diagonally to make a triangular-shaped pocket. Fill with the mixture and continue folding in. this triangular shape until all folded. Stick the end down with a little water or prepare a starch with cornflour and boiling water and use to glue the flaps.

Heat oil and deep fry Samoosa until golden. Drain and serve hot with mint chutney.

FRIED VEGETABLE DUMPLINGS

PAKORA

2 large potatoes
2 medium onions
5 spring onions
1 green chilli
1 medium eggplant, or 185 g (6 oz) spinach or cabbage
2 tomatoes
185 g (6 oz) gram flour *(besan)*
2 tablespoons self-raising flour
2 teaspoons salt
2 teaspoons *garam masala*
3 cm (1¼ inch) piece fresh ginger, minced
oil for deep frying

Peel potato, parboil and cut into very small dice. Finely chop onions, spring onions, chilli, eggplant, spinach or cabbage, and tomatoes. Mix with gram flour, self-raising flour, salt, *garam masala* and ginger. Mix to a smooth batter, adding just enough water to make it dropping consistency. Heat oil for deep frying and drop walnut-sized pieces of the batter into the oil and cook to a deep golden brown.

Drain well, then serve with mint chutney.

COLD LENTIL CAKES IN YOGHURT SAUCE

250 g (½ lb) yellow lentils, soaked overnight
1 medium onion
2 teaspoons salt
2 teaspoons *garam masala*
½ teaspoon chilli powder
2 teaspoons baking powder
pinch of asafoetida (optional)
ghee or oil for deep frying
2½ cups plain yoghurt
1 tablespoon thick cream (optional)
salt
pepper
sugar
2 teaspoons finely chopped mint

Rinse lentils and drain well. Put into a heavy duty grinder and grind to a smooth paste. It may be necessary to add a little water to prevent machine clogging. Mince onion and add to the lentil paste with salt, *garam*

Shrimp Rice (recipe page 20), Spiced Chickpeas (recipe page 18), and Dhal Special (recipe page 18).

masala, chilli powder, baking powder and asafoetida (if used). Mix thoroughly, then form the paste into walnut sized balls using wet or greased hands. If needed add a little plain flour or gram flour *(besan)* to bind.

Heat oil and drop in several balls at a time. Deep fry to a light golden brown. Lift out and drain thoroughly. Fry a second time for about 2 minutes on moderate heat and drain well.

Whip yoghurt with cream (if used) and season with salt, pepper and sugar to taste. Place lentil cakes in a serving dish and pour on the yoghurt sauce. Garnish with chopped mint. Chill slightly, leaving for at least 1 hour before serving to allow lentil cakes to soften.

BAKED FISH WITH CREAMED TOMATO SAUCE

750 g (1½ lb) snapper, bream or other meaty fish
3 tablespoons *ghee*
1¼ teaspoons fenugreek, ground
4 cloves garlic, crushed
2.5 cm (1 inch) piece fresh ginger, minced
1 tablespoon coriander, ground
2 teaspoons cummin, ground
1½ teaspoons chilli powder
¾ teaspoon turmeric powder
6 medium tomatoes, peeled
¾ cup water or fish stock
½ cup thick cream
¼ cup plain yoghurt
salt
black pepper
lemon juice

Clean fish, remove scales and clip fins. Wipe dry.

Heat *ghee* in a small saucepan. Fry fenugreek, garlic and ginger in the *ghee* for 3 minutes, then add coriander, cummin, chilli and turmeric. Fry for 2 minutes, stirring frequently.

Chop tomatoes finely and add to the pan with water or stock. Cover and simmer until sauce is thick and creamy. Add cream and yoghurt and season to taste with salt and black pepper. Keep warm.

Sprinkle fish with salt, pepper and lemon juice and place in a lightly oiled oven-proof dish. Cover with a piece of foil and bake in a moderately hot oven for 15 minutes. Remove foil and cook for a further 5 minutes. Remove from the oven. Pour on hot sauce and return to the oven for 5 minutes before serving.

FISH KEBABS

500 g (1 lb) meaty white fish
1 cm (½ inch) piece fresh ginger, minced
2 tablespoons boiling water
¾ cup plain yoghurt
1 teaspoon fennel seeds, crushed
1 teaspoon cummin, ground
¼ teaspoon black pepper
1½ teaspoons chilli powder
pinch of ground cloves
2 curry leaves (optional)
1 teaspoon salt

1 large onion
1 green pepper
2 limes
lime or lemon juice
dry green mango powder *(amchur)*
ghee

Cut fish into 2 cm (¾ inch) cubes. Pour boiling water over ginger and leave for 10 minutes, then strain liquid over fish. Leave for 20 minutes. Mix yoghurt with fennel, cummin, pepper, chilli powder, clove powder, crumbled curry leaves (if used) and salt and rub into the fish pieces. Marinate for 2 hours.

Cut onion into thin slices and pull into rings. Cut pepper into thin circles. Cut lemons into wedges and place with onion and pepper on a serving plate. Thread fish onto skewers and brush with a little melted *ghee*. Roast over a charcoal fire or under the griller until cooked through but do not overcook. Sprinkle with dried mango powder and place on the plate with onion, pepper and limes. Serve hot.

GOAN CURRIED FISH

750 g (1½ lb) white fish fillets
1 tablespoon lemon juice
5 dried chillies, soaked
1 teaspoon cummin seeds
3 teaspoons coriander seeds
60 g (2 oz) grated fresh or desiccated coconut
6 cloves garlic
1 small onion
2 medium onions
3 cm (1¼ inch) piece fresh ginger
4 tablespoons *ghee* or 3 tablespoons coconut oil
¾ teaspoon turmeric powder
2 green chillies, thinly sliced
1 tablespoon finely chopped fresh coriander leaves
1½ tablespoons tamarind
1½ cups water
salt
sugar to taste

Cut fish into 5 cm (2 inch) pieces and sprinkle with lemon juice.

Grind ingredients from chillies to small onion to a paste. Thinly slice medium onions and shred ginger. Fry in *ghee* or oil for 4 minutes, then put in spicy coconut paste and fry for 2 minutes. Add turmeric, sliced chillies and chopped coriander. Infuse tamarind in water, strain and add to pan. Bring to the boil, reduce heat and simmer for 15 minutes.

Add sliced fish and cook gently for about 6 minutes. Season to taste with salt and sugar. Serve at once.

PRAWNS IN GREEN MASALA

750 g (1½ lb) raw prawns, in shells
2 medium onions
2 cloves garlic
2.5 cm (1 inch) piece fresh ginger
1 teaspoon fennel
½ teaspoon cummin
2 green chillies

5 tablespoons chopped fresh coriander leaves
1 teaspoon salt
2 tablespoons *ghee* or coconut oil
¾ cup water

Peel prawns, leaving heads and tails on. Slice one onion thinly and make a seasoning paste by grinding remaining onion with all other ingredients except *ghee* or oil.

Fry sliced onion in *ghee* or oil until soft, then add seasoning paste and fry for 4 minutes. Add water and simmer until sauce is thick and smooth. Put in prawns and cook for about 5 minutes, or until tender. Do not overcook. Check seasonings and serve at once.

Thinly sliced fish fillets may also be cooked in this sauce.

CHICKEN KASHMIR

DUM MURGHI KASHMIR

This chicken is cooked in two stages: marinated and roasted, then rubbed with a spice paste and fried.

1.5 kg (3 lb) chicken
6 cloves garlic
2.5 cm (1 inch) piece fresh ginger
1 green chilli
1 tablespoon lemon juice
1 teaspoon *garam masala*
1 teaspoon chilli powder
½ teaspoon salt
¼ teaspoon turmeric powder
½ cup plain yoghurt
½ teaspoon sugar

Clean the chicken and wipe dry. Grind all ingredients except yoghurt and sugar to a paste, then stir in yoghurt and sugar. Rub over the chicken, inside and out. Leave for 2 hours to absorb the flavours. Roast in a moderate oven until almost cooked through, then remove from oven and leave to cool completely.

Curry paste:
1 large onion
4 cloves garlic
2.5 cm (1 inch) piece fresh ginger
6 cloves
1 teaspoon black peppercorns
2.5 cm (1 inch) stick cinnamon
1 heaped teaspoon fennel seeds
2 tablespoons coriander
6 black cardamoms
1 teaspoon cummin
45 g (1½ oz) ground almonds
1 teaspoon salt
¼ cup plain yoghurt
¼ teaspoon saffron powder
2 tablespoons boiling water
1 teaspoon *garam masala*
1 tablespoon finely chopped fresh coriander leaves
4 tablespoons *ghee*

Mince onion with garlic and ginger. Grind all spices to a fine powder and mix with onion paste. Add almonds, salt, yoghurt and saffron steeped in boiling water. Rub this mixture over the chicken.

Add *ghee* to the pan and cook chicken, basting frequently with *ghee* and the sauce, until chicken is done.

Sprinkle with *garam masala* and chopped coriander leaves before serving.

TANDOORI CHICKEN

6 chicken thighs
1 small onion, grated
3 cloves garlic, minced
juice of 1 lemon
2 teaspoons salt
3 dried chillies
1 teaspoon turmeric powder
1 teaspoon fenugreek seeds, ground
3 teaspoons coriander
1½ teaspoons cummin
1½ teaspoons black mustard seeds
2 teaspoons chilli powder
½ teaspoon red colouring powder
¾ cup plain yoghurt
softened *ghee*
dried green mango powder (*amchur*)
lemon wedges
onion rings

Prick chicken thighs with a skewer and remove skin. Rub with a mixture of grated onion, garlic, lemon juice and salt. Leave for 20 minutes.

Grind chillies with remaining spices and mix with red colouring powder and yoghurt. Rub this mixture well into the chicken, cover and leave overnight.

Brush with *ghee* and bake in a moderately hot oven or under a moderate grill until cooked through. Brush with more *ghee* during cooking.

Sprinkle with mango powder and serve with lemon wedges and onion rings.

CHICKEN PILLAU

375 g (¾ lb) long grain rice
750 g (1½ lb) chicken
2 medium onions
3 cloves garlic, minced
6 tablespoons *ghee*
4 cm (1½ inch) piece fresh ginger, minced
½ cup plain yoghurt
2 teaspoons salt
½ teaspoon ground black pepper
2 bay leaves
5 cm (2 inch) stick cinnamon
4 black cardamoms, crushed
pinch of freshly grated nutmeg
2 fresh red chillies
4 shallots

Wash rice in cold water and drain well. Cut chicken into 2.5 cm (1 inch) cubes. Slice one onion and mince the other. Heat 5 tablespoons *ghee* and fry sliced onion until soft. Add minced onion and garlic and fry for 2 minutes, then put in chicken pieces and cook until well coloured.

Add ginger and yoghurt, stirring well. Pour rice into the pan and add salt, pepper, bay leaves, cinnamon, cardamoms and nutmeg. Cover to 3 cm (1¼ inches) above the level of the rice with water or light chicken stock. Cover and bring to the boil. Reduce heat and simmer until the rice is tender and chicken cooked through.

Fry sliced chillies and shallots in 1 tablespoon *ghee* or oil for 2 minutes and stir into rice.

KEBABS OF MINCED LAMB

SHEEK KEBAB

750 g (1½ lb) boneless lamb, finely minced
¼ teaspoon saffron powder
2 tablespoons water
2 teaspoons cummin, ground
1 large onion, minced
3 cloves garlic, crushed
2½ tablespoons finely chopped fresh coriander leaves
1½ teaspoons salt
3 tablespoons *ghee*
dried green mango powder *(amchur)*
lettuce leaves
lime wedges
onion rings

Mix all ingredients except 1 tablespoon *ghee* and dried green mango powder together and knead until smooth. Divide into 5 cm (2 inch) balls and flatten each into a sausage shape. Insert a flat metal skewer along each kebab, press firmly onto the skewer and roll across the bottom of a plate to give an even shape.

Melt remaining *ghee* and brush each kebab lightly. Cook under a hot grill or on a charcoal barbecue until well browned on the surface and cooked through. Brush with more *ghee* during cooking to keep moist. Remove from heat and sprinkle with mango powder.

Serve with lime wedges and onion rings on a bed of lettuce leaves.

MUTTON IN COCONUT CURRY

750 g (1½ lb) mutton shoulder
1 teaspoon salt
3 cups thin coconut milk
4 cloves garlic, sliced
1 cm (½ inch) piece fresh ginger, shredded
6 dried chillies, soaked and mashed
½ teaspoon turmeric powder
10 cm (4 inch) stalk lemon grass, quartered
4 curry leaves
¾ teaspoon fenugreek seeds, crushed
5 cm (2 inch) stick cinnamon
1 medium onion, sliced
1 cup thick coconut milk
salt
lemon juice
1 tablespoon coconut oil or *ghee*

Trim mutton and cut into 2.5 cm (1 inch) cubes. Sprinkle with salt and place in a saucepan. Pour on thin coconut milk and add garlic, ginger and mashed chillies. Colour with turmeric powder and add half each of lemon grass, curry leaves, fenugreek seeds and cinnamon stick. Add sliced onion, reserving a little for gar-

nish. Cover and simmer until lamb is tender, stirring occasionally.

Add thick coconut milk and season to taste with salt and lemon juice. Heat *ghee* and fry remaining lemon grass, crumbled curry leaves, fenugreek seeds, cinnamon stick and onion for 4 minutes. Stir into the curry and cook for a further 15 minutes on low heat.

SAVOURY MINCED MEAT

RESHMI KIMA

250 g (½ lb) boneless mutton
6 cloves garlic
1 small onion
2.5 cm (1 inch) piece fresh ginger
½ cup water
2 tablespoons *ghee*
1 teaspoon salt
1 teaspoon *garam masala*
pinch of chilli powder
pinch of black pepper
1 tablespoon finely chopped fresh coriander leaves

Mince mutton with garlic, onion and ginger. Boil with water until all liquid has dried up and meat is well coloured. Add *ghee*, salt, *garam masala*, chilli powder and black pepper and fry for 5 minutes, stirring frequently. Add coriander and mix in well.

Serve with Chupati or fresh toast as a snack or breakfast dish.

MUTTON BIRIYANI

375 g (¾ lb) lean mutton
¼ cup plain yoghurt
2 teaspoons lemon juice
4 teaspoons *garam masala*
1 teaspoon turmeric powder
4 cloves garlic
1 large onion
2.5 cm (1 inch) piece fresh ginger
3 tablespoons *ghee*
375 g (¾ lb) long grain rice
2 medium onions, thinly sliced
5 cm (2 inch) cinnamon stick, broken
4 cloves
2 blades mace
3 bay leaves
½ teaspoon chilli powder
3 hardboiled eggs
1 tablespoon blanched almonds, fried in *ghee*

Trim mutton and cut into 3 cm (1¼ inch) cubes. Place in a bowl and pour on yoghurt and lemon juice. Sprinkle on 2 teaspoons *garam masala* and the turmeric. Finely mince garlic, onion and ginger and add to the meat. Stir well and leave to marinate for 1 hour.

Put marinated mixture into a pan, cover with water and boil for 1½ hours. Drain, reserving stock.

Heat *ghee* and fry rice until each grain is well oiled. Add onion, cinnamon, cloves, mace and bay leaves. Fry for 3 minutes then add drained meat and fry until well coloured. Pour in mutton stock and add water, if

Chicken Kashmir (recipe page 13).

needed, to make up 3¼ cups. Add chilli powder and bring to the boil. Cover and reduce heat to lowest point. Leave to cook until rice is tender and liquid completely absorbed.

Sprinkle on *garam masala* and stir meat into the rice. Cut hardboiled eggs into wedges and decorate the rice with egg and almonds. Serve hot.

DHANSAK WITH BROWN RICE

375 g (¾ lb) mixed lentils (black, yellow, red, chickpeas, etc)
750 g (1½ lb) lamb shoulder or leg
90 g (3 oz) pumpkin
125 g (¼ lb) spinach
1 large onion
3 tablespoons chopped fresh coriander leaves
2 teaspoons turmeric powder
2 teaspoons salt
4 dried chillies, soaked
2 teaspoons tamarind
3 tablespoons boiling water
2.5 cm (1 inch) piece fresh ginger
6 cloves garlic
2 green chillies
3 cloves
5 cm (2 inch) stick cinnamon
3 green cardamoms
1 teaspoon black mustard seeds
1 tablespoon ground coriander
2 teaspoons ground cummin
3 tablespoons chopped fresh coriander leaves
salt
pepper
1 large onion, finely chopped
3 tablespoons *ghee*

If using hard lentils like black or green lentils or chickpeas, soak overnight, then boil for 3 hours to soften. Place all lentils, well washed, into a saucepan and add meat cut into 1 cm (½ inch) dice. Cover with water to 8 cm (3 inches) above the level of the ingredients and bring to the boil. Simmer for at least 1 hour.

Peel and slice pumpkin, chop spinach and slice onion. Add pumpkin, spinach, coriander leaves, onion, turmeric and salt to the pan and cook until meat and lentils are tender. Remove meat and place in another pan. Mash lentils with vegetables or put in a blender to puree.

Grind seasonings (from dried chillies to green chillies) to a paste. Soak tamarind in water and add to paste together with cloves, cinnamon, cardamom and mustard seeds. Add ground coriander and cummin.

Heat *ghee* and fry seasonings for 4 minutes, then add fresh coriander, salt, pepper and finely chopped onion. Cook for a further 3 minutes, then put in lamb and cook until well coloured. Add lentil puree and adjust seasoning to taste. Heat through.

Keep warm while rice is prepared.

Brown Rice:
315 g (10 oz) long grain rice
2 large onions
2 tablespoons *ghee*
4 cloves

2 black cardamoms
5 cm (2 inch) stick cinnamon
salt
sugar
pepper

Wash rice and drain well. Chop onions finely and fry in *ghee* until very well coloured. They should be very dark brown, almost black. Add spices and rice and cover with water to 3 cm (1¼ inch) above the rice. Cover and bring to the boil. Simmer until cooked through. Season to taste with salt, pepper and sugar.

BRAISED LAMB WITH FRUIT AND NUTS

750 g (1½ lb) boned young lamb, leg or shoulder
3 cups water
1 tablespoon lemon juice
2 bay leaves
5 cm (2 inch) stick cinnamon
4 tablespoons *ghee*
5 cm (2 inch) piece fresh ginger, shredded
6 cloves garlic, crushed
2 large onions, minced
6 green cardamoms, crushed
2 tablespoons coriander, ground
3 cloves
1 tablespoon white poppy seeds
45 g (1½ oz) ground almonds
1 teaspoon black pepper
2 tablespoons finely chopped fresh mint
¾ cup plain yoghurt
2 teaspoons *garam masala*
1 teaspoon chilli powder
salt
45 g (1½ oz) raisins, soaked
30 g (1 oz) sultanas, soaked
45 g (1½ oz) blanched, slivered almonds
¼ teaspoon saffron
1 tablespoon boiling water
1½ teaspoons rose water (optional)

Place trimmed lamb in a pot and add water, lemon juice, bay leaves and cinnamon. Cover and bring to the boil, then reduce heat and simmer for about 1 hour until very tender. Skim several times during cooking. Remove meat and reduce liquid to about ¾ cup.

Heat 3 tablespoons *ghee* and fry ginger, garlic and onions until soft. Grind cardamoms, coriander, cloves, poppy seeds, almonds and black pepper to a powder and add to the pan. Fry for 3 minutes, stirring frequently. Add mint and yoghurt and simmer until sauce is thick and creamy.

Add the meat and spoon the sauce over it. Braise until heated through and well seasoned. Add reserved stock and simmer uncovered, until the liquid is completely absorbed or evaporated. Sprinkle on *garam masala*, chilli powder and salt.

Melt remaining *ghee* and fry drained fruit and nuts gently for 5 minutes. Add to the pan. Mix saffron with boiling water and rose water. Pour over the meat and heat through, or cover and place in a moderate oven for 15 minutes.

MUTTON KORMA

750 g (1½ lb) lean shoulder of mutton
2 large onions
2 cloves garlic
4 tablespoons *ghee*
2.5 cm (1 inch) piece fresh ginger
1 tablespoon coriander, ground
2 teaspoons cummin, ground
3 cloves
3 black cardamoms
5 cm (2 inch) stick cinnamon
2 teaspoons chilli powder
pinch of asafoetida (optional)
1 tablespoon white poppy seeds, soaked overnight
2 bay leaves
¾ cup plain yoghurt
salt
pepper
¾ cup thick cream
1 tablespoon raisins, soaked
3 tablespoons blanched almonds
1 teaspoon rose water
1 teaspoon saffron powder
2 tablespoons boiling water

Trim mutton and cut into 5 cm (2 inch) cubes. Slice onion thinly and crush garlic. Fry in 3 tablespoons of *ghee* until soft. Shred ginger and add to the pan with mutton cubes. Fry until well coloured, turning frequently. Add coriander and all spices to bay leaves and stir on moderate heat for 3 minutes.

Pour in yoghurt and stir to coat the meat thoroughly and mix with the spices. Cover and simmer until meat is tender and liquid completely absorbed. Splash in a little water and add salt and pepper. Add thick cream and raisins and cover again. Continue to simmer until meat is very tender and sauce thick. Add a little more water if needed.

Fry almonds in 1 tablespoon *ghee* until golden and stir into the sauce. Add rose water and saffron mixed with boiling water. Heat through for 10 minutes on low heat.

BEEF VINDALOO

1 kg (2 lb) beef steak (chuck, round or knuckle) or
    1½ kg (3 lb) oxtail
3 tablespoons coriander
1 tablespoon cummin
6 cloves
5 cm (2 inch) stick cinnamon
1½ teaspoons black peppercorns
2 teaspoons fenugreek seeds
1 teaspoon fennel seeds
6 dried chillied, soaked
8 cloves garlic
1 large onion
2.5 cm (1 inch) piece fresh ginger
¼ cup white vinegar
3 tablespoons *ghee*
2 bay leaves
2 cups beef stock
salt to taste

Trim meat and cut into 5 cm (2 inch) cubes. Set aside. Grind spices from coriander to fennel to a fine powder. Grind chillies with garlic, onion and ginger. Mix spice powder with vinegar and rub well into the meat. Pour on the onion paste and leave meat to marinate for 2 hours.

Heat *ghee* and fry meat until very deeply coloured. Add bay leaves and stock bring to the boil, then simmer until meat is very tender. Season to taste with salt and leave overnight if time permits. Reheat before using.

If using oxtail, cut into sections and prepare in the same way, cooking until the meat falls from the bones.

SPICED PORK

ASSAD

750 g (1½ lb) pork shoulder
salt
2.5 cm (1 inch) piece fresh ginger
8 cloves garlic
1 teaspoon turmeric powder
¼ teaspoon white pepper
3 tablespoons *ghee*
5 cm (2 inch) stick cinnamon
3 cloves
6 dried chillies
2 blades mace
1½ cups water

Wipe pork and trim. Rub with a little salt. Grind ginger and garlic to a paste with turmeric and pepper and rub into the pork. Heat *ghee* and fry meat until well coloured all over.

Transfer to a deep pot and add spices and water. Cover and bring to the boil. Simmer until meat is completely tender. Lift out and drain. Slice thickly before serving.

GOAN MEAT CURRY

SORPOTEL

This is a famous dish from Goa which should be prepared several days in advance to bring out the full flavour.

750 g (1½ lb) pork, slightly fatty
250 g (½ lb) pigs liver (in one piece)
1 tablespoon coriander
1½ teaspoons cummin
1 teaspoon black peppercorns
3 tablespoons malt vinegar
1 teaspoon turmeric powder
3 green chillies
4 cloves garlic
1 cm (½ inch) piece fresh ginger
3 tablespoons *ghee*
2 teaspoons tamarind or lemon juice to taste
sugar
salt

Cut pork into reasonably large pieces and place in a saucepan with the piece of liver. Cover with water to just above the level of the meat and bring to the boil. Reduce heat and simmer for about 1½ hours until pork is tender. Remove meat, retaining the stock. Cut meat and liver into 1 cm (½ inch) dice.

Toast coriander, cummin and peppercorns under the griller for 3 minutes, then grind to a fine powder. Mix with vinegar and add turmeric. Mince chillies with garlic and ginger and fry in *ghee* for 3 minutes. Add spice powder and meat and fry until meat is well coloured.

Add the reserved stock and tamarind or lemon juice, and boil for 45 minutes, or until meat is very tender and liquid well reduced. Season to taste with sugar and salt and heat through again. Leave to cool, then cover and refrigerate for at least one day, but preferably up to three days before using.   Reheat before serving.

CURRIED LIVER

375 g (¾ lb) lambs liver
1 medium onion
2 cloves garlic
2 green chillies
2 tablespoons *ghee*
½ teaspoon turmeric powder
2 teaspoons *garam masala*
2 cloves
2 bay leaves
pinch of white pepper
2 medium tomatoes, peeled
salt
¼ cup cream or thick coconut milk
1 tablespoon finely chopped fresh coriander leaves

Trim liver and cut into thin slices. Peel and thinly slice onion, garlic and chillies. Heat *ghee* and fry liver and sliced ingredients for 4 minutes. Sprinkle on turmeric and *garam masala* and add cloves, bay leaves and white pepper. Sprinkle on a very little water and add thinly sliced tomato. Simmer until tomato is soft and liver lightly cooked. Add salt to taste and pour on cream or coconut milk. Stir well and heat through.

Stir in coriander leaves and serve at once.

CURRIED EGGS

8 large eggs
2 tablespoons *ghee*
5 shallots, thinly sliced
2 cloves garlic, crushed
1 green chilli, chopped
1 cm (½ inch) piece fresh ginger, shredded
2 teaspoons dried prawns, soaked and ground
½ teaspoon fennel seeds
1 teaspoon fenugreek seeds, lightly crushed
1 teaspoon turmeric powder
1½ cups thin coconut milk
½ cup thick coconut milk
lemon juice
salt
pepper
1 tablespoon finely chopped fresh coriander leaves

Place eggs in a pan of cold water and boil for 10

minutes. Run eggs under cold water, peel, cover with cold water and set aside. Heat *ghee* and fry shallots and garlic until soft. Add chilli, ginger, dried prawns, fennel and fenugreek and fry for 4 minutes, stirring frequently. Sprinkle on turmeric and add whole or halved boiled eggs. Turn to coat evenly with the seasonings, and fry for 3 minutes.

Pour on thin coconut milk and simmer for 10 minutes, then add thick coconut milk and season to taste with lemon juice, salt and pepper. Heat through and stir in chopped coriander.

DHAL SPECIAL

250 g (½ lb) red or yellow lentils
2 medium onions
2 cloves garlic
1 green chilli
3 tablespoons *ghee*
1 tablespoon coriander, ground
1 teaspoon turmeric powder
1 teaspoon cummin, ground
salt
pepper
¼ cup thick cream
2 teaspoons coriander seeds
4 shallots, thinly sliced
1 tablespoon *ghee*

Wash lentils and cover with water to about 4 cm (1½ inches) above the level of the lentils. Bring to the boil and cook until very soft, then drain well, reserving the liquid.

Mince onions, garlic and chilli and fry in *ghee* for 3 minutes. Add spices and fry for 2 minutes, then pour in lentil mixture and heat through. Mash to a smooth puree and season to taste with salt and pepper. Stir in cream and some of the reserved liquid if too thick. The Dhal should have the consistency of a thick soup.

Fry coriander seeds and sliced shallots in *ghee* for 1 minute and stir into the Dhal.

SPICED CHICKPEAS

KABLI CHANNA

625 g (1¼ lb) canned chickpeas
1 large onion
5 cm (2 inch) piece fresh ginger
2 cloves garlic
3 tablespoons *ghee*
1 teaspoon pomegranate seeds, ground, or
    1 tablespoon lemon juice
1½ teaspoons *garam masala*
¾ teaspoon dried green mango powder *(amchur)*
2 green chillies, sliced
2 large tomatoes, peeled
3 tablespoons chopped fresh coriander leaves
salt
black pepper
chilli powder (optional)

Drain chickpeas, reserving a little of the liquid. Slice onion thinly. Shred or grate ginger and crush garlic. Fry

Braised Lamb with Fruit and Nuts (recipe page 16).

onion, ginger and garlic in *ghee* until soft then add pomegranate seeds (if using lemon juice do not add at this point), *garam masala* and mango powder. Stir on moderate heat for 1 minute then put in drained chickpeas. Stir until well coated with the spices. Add sliced chillies and pour in the reserved chickpea liquid and enough water to just cover. Bring to the boil, reduce heat, and simmer for 10 minutes.

Chop tomatoes coarsely and add to the pan with coriander leaves, salt, pepper and lemon juice (if used). Continue to cook for a further 15 minutes.

Garnish with chilli powder. Leave overnight if time allows, and reheat before serving, for extra flavour.

SHRIMP RICE

375 g (¾ lb) long grain rice
1 large onion
4 tablespoons *ghee*
2 cloves garlic
2.5 cm (1 inch) piece fresh ginger
250 g (½ lb) raw shrimps, peeled
½ teaspoon ground black pepper
3 cloves
5 cm (2 inch) cinnamon stick
2 green cardamoms, crushed
1 teaspoon salt
¼ cup thick coconut milk or thick cream
1 bay leaf
fresh mint or coriander leaves
red or green chilli, sliced

Wash rice and soak in cold water for 40 minutes. Drain well. Slice onion thinly and fry in *ghee* until soft. Add minced garlic and ginger and fry for 1 minute, then put in shrimps and cook until pink. Add rice and stir on moderate heat until all grains are well coated with the *ghee*. Add pepper, cloves, cinnamon, cardamoms, salt and coconut milk or thick cream. Pour on water to reach 3 cm (1¼ inches) above the level of the rice. Add bay leaf. Cover and bring to the boil, then reduce heat and cook until rice is tender and liquid absorbed.

Stir rice well, cover and place in warm oven for 15 minutes. Garnish with mint or coriander leaves and sliced chilli.

YELLOW RICE

345 g (11 oz) long grain rice
¾ teaspoon saffron strands
1 tablespoon boiling water
5 cm (2 inch) stick cinnamon
4 cloves
3 black cardamoms
3 cups water
2 tablespoons *ghee*
30 g (1 oz) raisins
30 g (1 oz) blanched almonds

Soak rice in cold water for ½ hour. Drain well. Steep saffron in boiling water and grind to release the colour. Pour rice into a saucepan and add saffron water, cinnamon, cloves and cardamoms. Pour on water and bring to the boil. Cover, reduce heat and simmer until rice is

tender and liquid absorbed. Transfer to a hot oven for 10 minutes.

Fry raisins and blanched almonds gently in *ghee* for 2 minutes. Stir into the rice and serve at once.

LEAVENED WHITE BREAD

NAAN

Makes 4-5.

250 g (½ lb) plain flour
1¼ teaspoons baking powder
½ teaspoon sugar
pinch of salt
⅓ - ½ cup plain yoghurt
1 tablespoon vegetable oil
1 egg

Sieve flour into a bowl and add baking powder, sugar and salt. Mix in ⅓ cup yoghurt, vegetable oil and the egg. Work with the fingers into a smooth, soft dough. Add extra yoghurt if the dough still feels slightly stiff. Knead for 5 minutes, then cover with a damp cloth and leave in a warm place to rise for 4 hours.

Heat a hotplate or heavy-based frying pan. Divide the dough into 4-5 pieces and with wet fingers pull into an elongated triangular shape. Wet one side and stick this down on the pan. Cook on moderate heat for about 1½ minutes, then turn pan over so the top of the bread is exposed directly to the heat. Cook until dark brown flecks appear and the bread is springy to the touch.

Keep in a cloth or covered box until needed.

WHOLEWHEAT UNLEAVENED BREAD

CHUPATI

Makes about 12.

250 g (½ lb) wholewheat flour *(atta)*
about ¾ cup warm water
ghee

Sieve flour into a bowl and add enough water to make a soft, workable dough. Knead for at least 6 minutes until dough is very soft and will lift from the board without sticking. Cover with a damp cloth and leave for 1 hour.

Divide dough into twelve pieces and roll into balls. Roll each piece out very thinly in a circular shape with a floured rolling pin. Stack between greaseproof paper.

Heat a heavy frying pan or hot plate and cook the Chupati on each side until brown flecks appear. Transfer to a hot grill until the Chupati blow up like a balloon. Spread with a little *ghee* then wrap in a cloth until needed.

EGGPLANT CURRY

500 g (1 lb) eggplant
1 teaspoon salt

1 teaspoon saffron powder
3 tablespoons *ghee* or oil
4 shallots, thinly sliced
3 cloves garlic, thinly sliced
2.5 cm (1 inch) piece fresh ginger, thinly sliced
8 dried chillies, toasted
2 teaspoons mustard seeds, toasted
2 teaspoons fish floss or dried shrimps, ground
10 cm (4 inch) stalk lemon grass
½ teaspoon fenugreek seeds, lightly crushed
1½ cups thin coconut milk
lemon juice
salt

Wipe eggplant and remove stems. Slice diagonally into 1 cm (½ inch) slices. Sprinkle with salt and leave for 10 minutes to draw bitter juices. Wipe off liquid and sprinkle slices with saffron powder.

Heat *ghee* or oil and fry eggplant until well coloured. Drain well. Fry shallots and garlic for 1 minute, then add ginger and chillies with all seasonings and stir on moderate heat for 1 minute. Pour in coconut milk and bring to a gentle boil. Simmer for 5 minutes. Add eggplant and cook until tender.

Season to taste with lemon juice and salt.

TOMATO PUREE

TAMATAR BURTHA

4 large tomatoes
2 large onions
1 clove garlic
1 green chilli
1 heaped teaspoon cummin, ground
1 teaspoon mustard seeds, toasted
1½ tablespoons *ghee*
1 tablespoon finely chopped fresh mint or coriander leaves
salt
sugar

Peel tomatoes and chop. Mince or finely chop onions, garlic and chilli. Heat oil and fry onion paste for 2 minutes, then add tomato with cummin and mustard. Simmer, stirring continually, until the mixture becomes a smooth sauce. Add a very little water if needed.

Stir in chopped mint or coriander leaves and season to taste with salt and sugar.

AUBERGINE PUREE

BRINJAL BURTHA

375 g (¾ lb) aubergines
2 medium onions
3 cloves garlic
2 tablespoons *ghee*
1 cm (½ inch) piece fresh ginger
2 teaspoons cummin, ground
1½ teaspoons *garam masala*
1½ teaspoons salt
2 spring onions, finely shredded
fresh coriander or mint leaves, finely chopped

Wipe eggplant and place under a moderate grill to cook until the skin is very dark and flesh completely soft. Peel off skin, discard stems and mash pulp or puree in a liquidiser.

Mince onions and garlic and fry in *ghee* for 2 minutes. Add minced ginger and eggplant puree and season with cummin. Simmer for 5 minutes on moderately low heat, then sprinkle on *garam masala* and salt. Add spring onion and cook for another 2 minutes.

Garnish with chopped coriander or mint.

DRY VEGETABLE CURRY

250 g (½ lb) cauliflower
3 medium potatoes
2 medium onions
125 g (¼ lb) green beans
2.5 cm (1 inch) piece fresh ginger
2 tablespoons *ghee*
1½ teaspoons salt
2 tomatoes
¾ teaspoon turmeric
½ teaspoon chilli powder
½ teaspoon mustard seeds
2 teaspoons *garam masala*

Break cauliflower into florets and rinse in cold water. Peel and cube potato. Slice onions thickly. Cut beans into 5 cm (2 inch) pieces. Shred ginger. Heat *ghee* and fry onions and ginger for 2 minutes. Add potato and cook until lightly coloured. Add cauliflower and beans with salt and cook briefly. Peel and slice tomato and add to the pan with turmeric, chilli powder and mustard seeds. Cover and cook until the vegetables are tender but retain some crispness.

Sprinkle on *garam masala* and cook, uncovered, until the liquid has dried up completely. Stir carefully to avoid breaking the vegetables.

MASALA POTATO WITH OKRA

2 large potatoes
250 g (½ lb) okra
3 green chillies
1 tablespoon fresh coriander leaves
1 large onion
1 large tomato
2 cloves garlic
1 cm (½ inch) piece fresh ginger
2 tablespoons *ghee*
2 teaspoons *chat masala* (see page 24)
½ teaspoon turmeric powder
1 cup water
sugar
salt

Peel potatoes and cut into 2.5 cm (1 inch) cubes. Wash okra and remove stems, slit lengthways. Cut green chillies into thin slices, removing seeds for milder taste. Chop coriander and slice onion and tomato. Crush garlic and shred ginger.

Heat *ghee* and fry sliced onion for 2 minutes. Add garlic and ginger and fry for a further 2 minutes, then sprinkle on *chat masala* and turmeric. Stir on high heat for 1 minute.

Add potatoes and okra and pour on water. Add chopped coriander leaves and tomato. Season to taste with sugar and salt and bring to the boil. Reduce heat and simmer until potatoes and okra are tender.

Serve with the sauce or cook until the liquid has almost evaporated.

SPICED POTATOES

ALOO CHAT

500 g (1 lb) potatoes, peeled
2½ tablespoons *ghee*
1 large onion, minced
2 cloves garlic, minced
2 teaspoons *chat masala* (see page 24)
1 teaspoon turmeric powder
1 teaspoon chilli powder
1½ teaspoons salt
1 bay leaf, crumbled
½ teaspoon freshly ground black pepper
1 fresh red chilli, finely chopped
1 tablespoon finely chopped fresh coriander leaves

Cut potatoes into 2.5 cm (1 inch) cubes. Heat *ghee* and fry potato until well coloured and slightly crisp. Add onion and garlic and cook for 1 minute. Sprinkle on spices and add bay leaf. Cover pan and cook on low heat until tender. If needed, sprinkle on a little water. Shake the pan to turn potatoes. Do not open saucepan until done.

Serve with a sprinkling of black pepper and garnish with chopped chilli and coriander leaves.

CREAM CURRY OF MUSHROOMS, PEAS AND TOMATO

SHABNAB

185 g (6 oz) canned champignons
185 g (6 oz) frozen green peas
6 medium tomatoes
3 tablespoons *ghee*
1½ teaspoons *garam masala*
¼ teaspoon fennel
pinch of salt and pepper
⅓ teaspoon turmeric powder
¾ cup thick cream
1 tablespoon finely chopped fresh coriander leaves
½ teaspoon chilli powder (optional)

Drain champignons. Thaw peas. Drop tomatoes into boiling water, count to eight and lift out. Peel and cut into wedges, discarding seeds if preferred.

Heat *ghee* and fry *garam masala* and fennel for 1 minute. Add tomato and fry until slightly softened. Add champignons and peas and cook briefly, then season with salt and pepper. Add turmeric and cream and simmer until heated through.

Stir in chopped coriander leaves and garnish with a sprinkling of chilli powder.

STUFFED LADIES FINGERS

BAHMIA

375 g (¾ lb) large okra
2 medium tomatoes
1 tablespoon brown sugar
2 tablespoons lemon juice
2 teaspoons fennel seeds, coarsely ground
¾ teaspoon turmeric powder
1 tablespoon coriander, ground
1 tablespoon *ghee*
salt
chilli powder
2 tablespoons beef stock

Wash okra, trim tops and cut a slit along each piece. Peel and finely chop tomato and mix with brown sugar, lemon juice and spices. Stuff the mixture into the okra and place in a fireproof dish.

Melt *ghee* and add to the dish. Sprinkle on salt and chilli powder and add beef stock. Cover and cook in a moderate oven or over moderate heat until the okra are tender, then remove lid and continue cooking until the pan juices are absorbed.

TOMATO AND ONION SALAD

LACHUMBER

3 medium tomatoes
2 medium onions
3 green chillies
vinegar or tamarind water
salt
sugar

Peel and finely chop tomatoes and onions. Slice chillies thinly, discarding seeds. Mix vinegar or tamarind water, salt and sugar to taste and pour over the vegetables. Leave to stand for 1 hour before serving.

Serve as a side dish with any main dishes.

YOGHURT SALAD WITH ONION AND MINT

RAITA

2 cups plain yoghurt
3 spring onions, minced
2 tablespoons finely chopped fresh mint
½ teaspoon salt
1 teaspoon sugar
¼ teaspoon black pepper
½ teaspoon cummin, ground

Beat yoghurt until smooth then stir in all remaining ingredients. Beat for 1 minute then refrigerate. Add 2 tablespoons thick cream for a richer sauce. Serve as a side dish with any main course.

Yoghurt side dishes may include any of the following ingredients: finely chopped tomato or pineapple, grated cucumber, cooked peas with mint, cooked finely diced potato, grated apple, chopped banana, or they can simply be flavoured with spices.

SPICES

With the exception of a few freshly made curry pastes purchased from local markets, few Indian cooks would consider using commercial curry powders or pastes in their cooking. Instead, each household is equipped with a spice grinder, either an electric appliance or the time honoured 'curry stone', a granite grinding stone and pestle. Whole fresh spices are ground just before using for maximum freshness. The most commonly used spice blend is garam masala, which is used in conjunction with other spices, or is used as a condiment and sprinkled on a cooked dish. Chat masala is a tart flavoured spice combination particularly good with vegetable dishes. Recipes for these two spice mixes are given below. They may be made in quantity and keep well in an airtight container.

GARAM MASALA

60 g (2 oz) black peppercorns
60 g (2 oz) cummin seeds
60 g (2 oz) coriander seeds
25 large black cardamoms, peeled
15 g (½ oz) cloves
15 g (½ oz) ground cinnamon

Blend these to a fairly fine powder and pour into a jar with a tight fitting lid. The spice mixture will be even more fragrant if the peppercorns, cummin and coriander are lightly toasted under the griller before grinding.

CHAT MASALA

30 g (1 oz) cummin seeds
1 tablespoon salt
pinch of asafoetida
3 teaspoons chilli powder
2 tablespoons dried green mango powder (*amchur*)
1 tablespoon crushed dried mint
2 teaspoons dried ginger powder

Lightly toast cummin with salt and asafoetida. Grind all ingredients to a fine powder and pour into a jar with a tight fitting lid.

MANGO PICKLE

AAM KA ACHAR

2 kg (4 lb) small unripe mangoes
2 tablespoons fenugreek seeds
3 teaspoons turmeric powder
½ teaspoon asafoetida
12 dried red chillies, soaked
500 g (1 lb) coarse salt
2 cups mustard oil

Cut mangoes in halves, lengthways, cutting through the stone which will still be soft if mangoes are sufficiently unripe. Mix spices with salt and about 4 tablespoons oil and cover one half of each mango with a thick layer of the paste. Press the other half on top. Arrange all stuffed mangoes in a wide-necked jar and sprinkle on any remaining spices. Cover jar and leave for 1 day.

Heat remaining mustard oil to lukewarm and pour onto the mangoes. Seal jars again and leave in a warm sunny place for 10 days, or place in a very low oven for 2 days, then keep in a warm cupboard for 1 month.

Store in a cool dry cupboard when ready.

COCONUT CHUTNEY

125 g (¼ lb) grated fresh coconut, or
  90 g (3 oz) moistened desiccated coconut
1 tablespoon white poppy seeds, ground
1 heaped tablespoon finely chopped fresh coriander
  mint or leaves
¾ teaspoon mustard seeds
pinch of chilli
pinch of saffron powder
1 teaspoon cummin, ground
salt
sugar
lemon juice

Pound coconut with poppy seeds and coriander or mint leaves to a coarse paste. Add mustard seeds, chilli and saffron and cummin and mix well. Season to taste with salt and pepper and add lemon juice to moisten.

Store in an airtight container in the refrigerator for up to 5 days.

FRESH MINT CHUTNEY

90 g (3 oz) fresh mint
1 small onion
1-2 green chillies, seeds removed
2 teaspoons sugar
salt
lemon juice

Wash mint and pick off leaves, discarding stems. Chop leaves finely. Mince onion and chillies and mix with mint, adding sugar and salt and lemon juice to taste. Pound all together to a smooth paste or puree in the liquidiser.

Serve with Samoosa or Pakora.

STEAMED YOGHURT SWEET

BARPHI DAHI

4 cups fresh whole milk
125 g (¼ lb) sugar
1 cup plain yoghurt
12 blanched, slivered almonds
15 g (½ oz) raisins
1 tablespoon *ghee*

Bring milk to boil and continue to cook until reduced by half. Stir in sugar and cook until dissolved. Beat yoghurt and add to the milk mixture. Pour into a buttered fireproof dish and cover with foil. Place in a dish of water in a moderately hot oven and cook until the pudding sets.

Fry almonds and raisins in *ghee* and sprinkle over the pudding. Cook for a further 5 minutes. Serve hot or well chilled.

MILK BALLS IN SUGAR SYRUP

GULAB JAMON

185 g (6 oz) full cream milk powder
2 tablespoons *ghee*
125 g (¼ lb) self-raising flour
1 teaspoon baking powder
vegetable oil for deep frying
315 g (10 oz) sugar
1¾ cups water
1½ teaspoons rose water

Mix milk powder with *ghee* and work to a crumbly texture. Add self-raising flour and baking powder and mix well, crumbling with the fingers. Mix in a very little water to make a very stiff dough. Wrap in a damp cloth and leave for 3 hours.

Break the dough and rub hard on a floured board into fine crumbs. Add sprinkling of water and form mixture into walnut-sized balls. Heat oil and deep fry balls to a light golden brown. Shake pan during cooking to colour the balls evenly. Lift out and drain well.

Pour sugar and water into a saucepan and bring to the boil. Simmer until very slightly sticky. Splash in rose water and add milk balls. Leave milk balls to soak in the syrup for at least ½ hour before serving. Serve warm or chilled.

CARROT DESSERT

GAJAR HALWA

750 g (1½ lb) carrots
8 cups milk
3 tablespoons full cream milk powder
5 cm (2 inch) stick cinnamon
125 g (¼ lb) raisins, soaked
3 black cardamoms, crushed lightly
½ teaspoon saffron powder
1 tablespoon boiling water
3 tablespoons *ghee* or butter
2 tablespoons honey
185 g (6 oz) sugar, or to taste
90 g (3 oz) blanched, slivered almonds
1½ teaspoons rose water
silver leaf to decorate (optional)

Scrape carrots, rinse, then grate finely. Put into a saucepan and pour on milk. Add milk powder and cinnamon stick. Bring to the boil and cook, stirring frequently, until the mixture has thickened and carrot is beginning to become very soft. Add drained raisins, cardamoms and saffron mixed with boiling water and continue to cook, stirring continually, until the mixture becomes a thick paste.

Add *ghee*, honey and sugar and cook again, stirring, until thick. Stir in blanched almonds and rose water. Spoon into a lightly buttered dish and smooth the top. Decorate with silver leaf if available. Leave to cool before serving, or serve hot.

RICE PUDDING

KHEER

90 g (3 oz) short grain rice
3¼ cups fresh whole milk
2 green cardamoms
75 g (2½ oz) sugar

Wash rice and soak for ½ hour in cold water. Bring milk to a rolling boil and pour in drained rice and cardamoms. Cover and simmer until rice is completely soft.

Stir in sugar and continue cooking for 5 more minutes. Serve hot or cold.

BUTTERY PEA FLOUR FUDGE

MYSORE PAK

440 g (14 oz) *ghee*
125 g (¼ lb) gram flour *(besan)*
315 g (10 oz) sugar
¾ cup water

Melt one-third of the *ghee* and fry flour until lightly coloured. Melt remaining *ghee* and set aside.

Pour sugar and water into a saucepan and bring to the boil. Cook without stirring until very sticky and beginning to darken. Test if right by dabbing a little on the back of a wooden spoon. Press a finger on and pull away. The toffee should form into long firm threads between finger and spoon.

Add fried flour and melted *ghee* and cook on moderate heat, stirring continually, until very thick.

Pour into a buttered square tray and press flat. Cut into squares when set and serve when completely cold.

COCONUT TOFFEE

NARIAL KI BARFI

125 g (¼ lb) desiccated coconut
155 g (5 oz) sugar
½ - ¾ cup water
1 green cardamom, ground
pink food colouring

Moisten coconut slightly with water. Pour sugar and water into a small saucepan and cook on low heat without stirring until the syrup is sticky. To test if ready dab a little onto the back of a wooden spoon. Press a finger onto it and draw away. When thin threads of toffee are formed between spoon and finger, syrup is the correct consistency. Add moistened coconut and stir until mixture is thick. Stir in cardamom.

Spread half onto a greased tray and colour the other half pink. Pour on top and press flat. Mark out squares before completely set and cut when cold.

INDONESIA

WRAPPED FISH
PANGGANG BUNGKUS

1 whole fish (pomfret, turbot or sole), weighing about
    410 g (13 oz)
1 teaspoon tamarind, crumbled
2 teaspoons salt
10 candlenuts, ground
¾ teaspoon turmeric powder
½ teaspoon dried shrimp paste
1 cm (½ inch) piece fresh ginger
2 fresh red chillies, finely chopped
1-2 teaspoons chilli powder
2 medium onions
1 clove garlic
1 *daun salam* or bay leaf
4 fresh basil leaves (optional)
banana leaf or aluminium foil
tomato wedges

Clean fish and score diagonally across both sides. Rub with salt and tamarind over skin and inside cavity. Grind candlenuts with turmeric, shrimp paste, ginger, fresh chillies and chilli powder. Chop onion and garlic finely and mix with the ground seasonings.

Coat the fish thickly with the seasoning paste and place *daun salam* or bay leaf and basil (if used), inside cavity.

Hold banana leaf over a flame to soften. Brush with oil. Wrap fish in banana leaf or foil, securing with toothpicks or tieing with cotton. Roast over a charcoal fire or in a moderate oven for about 15-20 minutes.

Test if fish is done by inserting a thin skewer in the thickest part. If the flesh is tender and no pink juices escape, the fish is ready. To serve, tear away the top part of the banana leaf or foil wrapping. Place on a wooden plate and surround with tomato wedges.

SPICED FISH
IKAN PECAL

500 g (1 lb) thick fillets of cod, snapper or haddock
3 medium onions
3 cloves garlic
1 tablespoon chilli powder
½ teaspoon sweet basil, powdered or flaked
1 cm (½ inch) piece fresh ginger, shredded
½ teaspoon dried shrimp paste
4 candlenuts, ground
1 small piece tamarind
2 teaspoons salt
1 cup thick coconut milk
lemon or lime wedges

Chop or mince onion and garlic finely. Mix all ingredients except lemon wedges together and blend well. Slice fish into 12 pieces and arrange in a flat bowl. Pour

on the marinade and stand for 20 minutes.

Remove from the liquid and grill fillets, basting with the marinade as they cook. When done, transfer to a warmed serving plate.

Bring the remaining marinade to the boil in a small saucepan and simmer until slightly thickened. Strain over fish. Serve with lemon or lime wedges.

SHRIMP CURRY
KARI UDANG

375 g (¾ lb) peeled raw shrimps
salt
pepper
1 cm (½ inch) piece fresh ginger, shredded
2 teaspoons chilli powder
1 teaspoon grated fresh turmeric, or
    ⅓ teaspoon turmeric powder
8 candlenuts, ground
1 tablespoon coconut oil
2.5 cm (1 inch) piece *lengkuas,* sliced (optional)
½ teaspoon dried shrimp paste
¾ cup fish stock
1½ cups thin coconut milk
1 stalk lemon grass
fresh coriander, chopped

Season shrimps with salt and pepper and fry in coconut oil until pink. Remove and set aside.

Grind ginger, chilli powder, turmeric and candlenuts to a paste and fry in oil for 3 minutes. Add sliced *lengkuas* and shrimp paste, then pour on fish stock and bring to the boil. Reduce heat and add coconut milk and lemon grass and boil briefly. Return shrimps and cook for 3-4 minutes on moderate heat.

Season with a salt and pepper to taste and garnish with chopped coriander.

FRIED CHILLI PRAWNS
SAMBAL GORENG UDANG

500 g (1 lb) large raw prawns in shells
salt
pepper
1 medium onion
2 small tomatoes
1½ tablespoons peanut oil
2 cloves garlic, crushed
2.5 cm (1 inch) piece *lengkuas,* minced
2-3 fresh red chillies, thinly sliced
2 teaspoons chilli powder
2.5 cm (1 inch) piece lemon grass
⅔ cup thin coconut milk
2 tablespoons tamarind water, made with ½ teaspoon
    tamarind
spring onions, chopped

Shrimp Curry (recipe this page).

Peel and devein prawns, leaving heads and tails attached. Season with salt and pepper.

Slice onion and tomato. Heat oil in a *wok* or saucepan and fry onion and garlic till soft. Add prawns and cook for 2 minutes. Add tomato, *lengkuas,* red chillies, chilli powder, lemon grass, salt and pepper. Cook for about 3 minutes, stirring occasionally. Turn heat down, pour on coconut milk and simmer for 3 minutes.

Strain tamarind and add liquid and chopped spring onions to the sauce. Heat through and serve immediately.

SPICED ROAST DUCK

BEBEK BETUTU

2 kg (4 lb) duck
2 medium onions
4 cloves garlic
5 cm (2 inch) piece fresh ginger
1 tablespoon coconut or vegetable oil
2 fresh red chillies, chopped
12 candlenuts, ground
2 black cardamoms, ground
1 teaspoon grated fresh turmeric or
 ½ teaspoon turmeric powder
1 teaspoon dried shrimp paste
2 teaspoons salt
1 teaspoon white pepper
banana leaves, or aluminium foil

Clean duck and wash. Wipe dry and set aside.

Mince onion, garlic and ginger and fry in oil for 3 minutes. Grind chilli, candlenuts, cardamom, turmeric, shrimp paste, salt and pepper to a paste and add to the pan, frying for a further 3 minutes.

Stuff into the duck and secure opening with toothpicks or sew up carefully. Rub duck with salt and pepper and a little oil and wrap in several layers of banana leaf or foil. Secure with toothpicks or tie with cotton.

Bake in a preheated moderate oven (180°C/350°F/Gas Mark 4) for 2 hours. If crisp skin is preferred, remove wrappings, turn heat up and bake for a further 10 minutes.

FRIED CHICKEN WITH TAMARIND

AYAM GORENG ASAM

750 g (1½ lb) chicken
salt
pepper
2 medium onions
3 cloves garlic
40 g (1½ oz) tamarind
½ cup boiling water
oil for deep frying
sweet soya sauce
krupuk or potato crisps

Clean chicken and cut into large pieces. Season with salt and pepper. Grate onions and crush garlic. Soak tamarind in boiling water. Arrange chicken pieces in a flat bowl, sprinkle on grated onion and garlic and strain on

tamarind water. Marinate for 20 minutes. Lift up, drain and pat dry with kitchen paper.

Heat oil until almost at smoking point and carefully lower in several pieces of chicken. Deep fry for 2 minutes, then remove from oil and return to marinade while remaining pieces are cooked. Marinate for at least 10 minutes the second time, then drain again and pat dry.

Return to the hot oil and cook again for 2 minutes. Marinate once more, then fry chicken another 2 minutes. It should be crisp on the surface and the meat tender and moist. Serve with soya sauce dip and a plate of freshly fried *krupuk* or potato crisps.

CHICKEN LIVERS IN COCONUT CREAM

HATI AYAM

375 g (¾ lb) chicken livers
2 tablespoons peanut oil
2 medium onions, chopped
3 cloves garlic, crushed
1 heaped teaspoon chilli powder
2 fresh red chillies, sliced
12 candlenuts, ground
2 teaspoons brown sugar
1½ teaspoons salt
¾ cup thin coconut milk
½ cup thick coconut milk
5 cm (2 inch) stalk lemon grass
lemon juice
fried onion flakes (see page 34)
parsley or mint, chopped

Clean chicken livers and cut in halves. Heat oil and fry onions and garlic until soft. Add livers and saute until no pink shows. Sprinkle on chilli powder, and add sliced chillies, ground candlenuts, sugar and salt. Stir well, then pour in thin coconut milk and thick coconut milk and add lemon grass.

Simmer until livers are very tender. Sprinkle on lemon juice to taste and serve garnished with fried onions and chopped parsley or mint.

CHICKEN IN COCONUT SAUCE

OPOR AYAM

440 g (14 oz) chicken pieces
2 teaspoons salt
½ teaspoon white pepper
1 medium onion
2.5 cm (1 inch) piece fresh ginger
2.5 cm (1 inch) piece *lengkuas*
2 cloves garlic, crushed
3 black cardamoms, crushed
1 heaped teaspoon coriander, ground
½ teaspoon dried shrimp paste
8 candlenuts, ground
2 tablespoons oil
1 cup chicken stock
½ cup thick coconut milk
2 heaped teaspoons brown sugar
fresh coriander leaf or shredded spring onion

Chop chicken into medium pieces. Season with salt and pepper. Finely chop onion, ginger and *lengkuas* and pound to a paste with garlic, cardamom, coriander, shrimp paste and candlenuts.

Heat oil and fry seasoning paste for 4 minutes, then add chicken pieces and cook till well coloured. Pour in chicken stock, stir well, cover and bring to the boil, then turn heat down and simmer until chicken is tender. Add a little more water or stock if needed.

Pour in coconut milk and sprinkle on brown sugar and cook until sauce thickens. Garnish with coriander leaf or shredded spring onion.

LAMB WITH COCONUT
GULAI KAMBING

750 g (1½ lb) shoulder of lamb
salt
white pepper
2 teaspoons brown sugar
½ teaspoon turmeric powder
2 heaped teaspoons chilli powder
1 fresh red chilli, chopped
1 teaspoon dried shrimp paste
3 medium onions
2 cloves garlic
2 tablespoons vegetable oil
75 g (2½ oz) freshly grated coconut or
    40 g (1½ oz) desiccated coconut
1½ cups coconut milk
fresh coriander sprigs

Cut lamb meat into 2.5 cm (1 inch) cubes and dust with salt and pepper. Grind brown sugar with turmeric, chilli powder, fresh chilli, and shrimp paste. Peel onions and garlic and chop finely.

Heat oil and fry onions and garlic until soft. Add ground seasonings and fry for 4 minutes. Toss in lamb and cook until well browned, then add coconut. Brown for 10 minutes, stirring continually to prevent coconut burning.

Pour in coconut milk, lower heat and simmer until meat is tender. Season to taste with salt and pepper. Garnish with sprigs of coriander.

BRAISED SPICED BEEF
SEMUR SAPI

625 g (1¼ lb) rump or sirloin steak
2 medium onions
4 cloves garlic
2 tablespoons oil
⅔ cup beef stock
½ teaspoon grated nutmeg
2 teaspoons mixed spice
1½ teaspoons brown sugar
1½ teaspoons salt
1 teaspoon white pepper
2 tablespoons sweet soya sauce
tomato wedges
onion flakes (see page 34)
fresh coriander leaves

Cut beef into 2.5 cm (1 inch) cubes, after removing any fat. Peel and chop onions and garlic. Heat oil in a pan and fry onions and garlic until light brown and soft. Put in beef, turn heat up slightly and fry for 5-6 minutes, turning to brown well. Pour in beef stock, cover and simmer for 10 minutes.

Add nutmeg, mixed spice, brown sugar, salt, pepper and sweet soya sauce. Reduce heat and cook until meat is tender, adding a little more water from time to time as liquid dries up.

Serve with tomato wedges and garnish with fried onion or sprigs of coriander.

COCONUT BEEF
DENDENG RAGI

500 g (1 lb) rump or sirloin steak
1 tablespoon coriander, ground
½ teaspoon powdered sweet basil, or
    2 teaspoons fresh basil, chopped
1 tablespoon brown sugar
2 teaspoons tamarind
3 cloves garlic, crushed
3 medium onions, grated
2 tablespoons oil
2 *daun salam* or bay leaves
155 g (5 oz) freshly grated coconut, or
    100 g (3½ oz) moistened desiccated coconut
salt
pepper

Slice beef thinly. Grind coriander, basil, brown sugar and tamarind to a paste and mix with garlic and onions.

Heat oil in a frying pan and fry seasoning paste for 5 minutes, stirring occasionally. Season beef with salt and pepper and add to the pan. Cook over high heat until very well browned. Remove and keep warm.

In a dry pan pour desiccated or grated coconut and add *daun salam* or bay leaves. Turn heat down low and stir coconut as it cooks. It burns very quickly, so do not stop stirring at any time. When coconut is lightly browned add meat and cook until warmed through.

SWEET PORK
BABI KECAP

625 g (1¼ lb) pork belly with rind
2 teaspoons salt
1 teaspoon white pepper
2 tablespoons plain flour
oil for deep frying
3 medium onions
2 cloves garlic
2 teaspoons tomato paste
3 tablespoons chicken stock
1½ tablespoons brown sugar
2½ tablespoons sweet soya sauce
fresh coriander leaves, chopped

Slice pork thinly. Sprinkle with salt and pepper and coat lightly with flour. Stand for 5 minutes.

Heat oil to smoking point and fry pork until well browned. Remove from oil, drain and set aside. Remove all but 1 tablespoon oil from pan.

Peel and chop onions and garlic and fry till soft. Add tomato paste, chicken stock and brown sugar and return pork slices. Sprinkle on sweet soya sauce and simmer for 10 minutes, adding a little water if the liquid dries up. Turn heat up slightly and cook for a further 5-7 minutes until all liquid is absorbed into the meat and pork is very tender.

Sprinkle on chopped coriander to garnish.

ROAST SUCKLING PIG

BABI GULING

4-5 kg (8-10 lb) suckling pig
10 cm (4 inch) piece fresh ginger, shredded
3 teaspoons turmeric powder
4 green cardamoms, crushed
1 tablespoon chilli powder
2 tablespoons salt
1 teaspoon grated nutmeg
3 teaspoons dried shrimp paste
1 stalk lemon grass, finely chopped
8 cloves
2 teaspoons black peppercorns
1 tablespoon tamarind
4 tablespoons vegetable oil
2 large onions, chopped
4 cloves garlic, crushed
salt
pepper

Have the butcher clean and prepare the piglet. Wash well and wipe dry.

Grind ginger, turmeric, cardamom, chilli, salt, nutmeg and shrimp paste. Add lemon grass, cloves, peppercorns and tamarind.

Heat oil and fry onion and garlic till soft. Add ground seasonings and fry for 4 minutes. Stuff into the prepared piglet and sew up opening. Rub skin with salt and pepper mixed with vegetable oil. Bake on a spit over a charcoal fire or in a moderately hot oven for 2½ hours. Test if the meat is done by inserting a skewer into the thickest part. If the liquid runs clear the piglet is cooked. Baste with oil during cooking.

Serve slices of pork with white rice and a hot tomato and chilli *sambal*.

If preparing a larger pig, increase the amounts of ingredients accordingly and allow extra cooking time.

CHILLI EGGS

TELUR BERLADO

6 large eggs
oil for deep frying
2 medium onions, minced
2 cloves garlic, minced
1 cm (½ inch) piece fresh ginger, minced
1 teaspoon dried shrimp paste
3 teaspoons chilli powder
2 fresh red chillies, finely chopped
5 cm (2 inch) stalk lemon grass, finely chopped
1 teaspoon tamarind
2 tablespoons boiling water
2 teaspoons sugar

¾ teaspoon turmeric powder
salt
pepper
fresh coriander leaves

Hardboil eggs and place in cold water. When cold remove shells and prick eggs with a fork to allow seasonings to penetrate. Heat oil and gently fry eggs to a deep golden colour and slightly crisp on the outside. Remove and set aside.

Pour off all but 1 tablespoon oil and fry onion, garlic and ginger for 2 minutes. Add shrimp paste, chilli powder, chopped chillies, lemon grass and tamarind mixed with boiling water. Stir over moderate heat for 2 minutes, then add sugar and turmeric. Stir well. Replace eggs and cook until the seasonings have dried up and cling to the eggs. Sprinkle on salt and pepper.

Serve eggs either whole or halved. Garnish with sprigs of fresh coriander.

FRIED NOODLES

BAKMI GORENG

250 g (½ lb) thin egg noodles
2 cloves garlic
1 large onion
vegetable oil
100 g (3½ oz) peeled raw shrimp
100 g (3½ oz) chicken, shredded
1 fresh red chilli, chopped
8 spring onions, chopped
100 g (3½ oz) Chinese cabbage, chopped
2 tablespoons dark soya sauce
2 teaspoons sugar
2 teaspoons salt
½ teaspoon white pepper
1 egg, beaten
dry fried onion flakes (see page 34)

Soak noodles for 10 minutes in cold water. Drain and spread on a tray to dry. Peel garlic and onion and chop finely. Fry in a little oil until soft. Put in shrimps and chicken and cook for 5 minutes. Add chilli, spring onions and cabbage and stir-fry for 3 minutes.

Mix soya sauce with sugar, salt and pepper and pour over the vegetables. Remove from heat and keep warm.

Pour 2 tablespoons oil into a pan and when hot fry noodles on high heat until lightly coloured and slightly crisped. Lift onto a serving dish. Reheat vegetable and meat topping and pour on.

Heat pan and fry beaten egg in a thin omelette, swirling pan to make it spread very thinly across the pan. Lift out, cool and shred.

Garnish the noodles with shredded egg and fried onion flakes and serve hot.

CHICKEN SOUP

SOTO AYAM

500 g (1 lb) chicken
2 medium onions
3 cloves garlic
1½ teaspoons coriander, ground

Coconut Beef (recipe page 29).

1 teaspoon turmeric powder
8 candlenuts, ground
½ teaspoon dried shrimp paste
3 tablespoons oil
salt
white pepper
60 g (2 oz) celery leaves, chopped
½ teaspoon tamarind
60 g (2 oz) cabbage, shredded
60 g (2 oz) beanshoots
4 cups water
60 g (2 oz) thin rice vermicelli
spring onions, chopped
fresh coriander sprigs

Cut chicken into several pieces. Put in a saucepan and cover with water. Peel and chop onions. Pound onion, garlic, coriander, turmeric, candlenuts and shrimp paste. Heat 1 tablespoon oil and fry ground seasonings for 4 minutes. Add to the chicken. Season with salt and pepper, add chopped celery leaves and simmer, covered, until chicken is tender.

Add tamarind, stir and continue to simmer for a few minutes. Remove pieces of chicken, strain stock, then return chicken and stock to pan.

Heat 2 tablespoons oil and fry cabbage and beanshoots lightly. Bring water to the boil in a large saucepan, add salt and vermicelli and cook till tender. Add vermicelli and fried vegetables to the chicken stock and heat through.

Garnish with chopped spring onions and coriander.

INDONESIAN FRIED RICE

NASI GORENG

4½ cups chicken stock
2 teaspoons tamarind
345 g (11 oz) rice
3 medium onions
4 cloves garlic
1 tablespoon oil
1 large tomato, sliced
1½ teaspoons dried shrimp paste
2 teaspoons chilli powder
100 g (3½ oz) lean beef, shredded
salt
white pepper
1 stalk celery, sliced
1 fresh red chilli, finely chopped
2 eggs
dry fried onion flakes (see page 34)

Bring stock to the boil and add the tamarind and well-washed rice. Boil for 12-15 minutes, or until rice is tender but not too soft. Drain, rinse in cold water and set aside to cool. Break up the tamarind and stir well to mix into the rice.

Peel and slice onions and garlic and fry in oil until soft. Add tomato, shrimp paste and chilli powder and cook for 2 minutes. Put in beef and season with salt and pepper. Saute for 3-4 minutes, stirring frequently. Add sliced celery and chopped chilli and cook for a further 2 minutes. Remove and set aside.

Wipe out pan and oil lightly. Beat eggs and pour into the pan. Cook in a thin omelette until set, then break up with a fork and add to the cooked beef mixture.

Add 2 tablespoons oil to the pan and stir-fry rice for 5 minutes, stir in cooked mixture and season with salt and pepper and a little soya sauce if desired.

Garnish with fried onion flakes.

MIXED VEGETABLES IN COCONUT SAUCE

SAYUR LODEH

1 medium potato
1 medium carrot
60 g (2 oz) green beans, sliced
100 g (3½ oz) cabbage, shredded
100 g (3½ oz) beanshoots
2 medium onions
2 cloves garlic
1 tablespoon oil
½ medium cucumber
1 teaspoon tamarind, crumbled
2.5 cm (1 inch) piece fresh ginger, minced
2 teaspoons coriander, ground
2 teaspoons salt
1½ cups thick coconut milk
krupuk

Peel and slice potato and carrot and parboil for 3 minutes. Add beans and cabbage and cook for 2 more minutes, then drain. Splash with cold water and allow to cool.

Steep beanshoots in boiling water for 2 minutes. Drain. Peel onion and garlic and chop finely. Fry in oil until soft. Slice cucumber thinly and saute with onions for 2 minutes.

Mix tamarind with ginger, coriander, salt and coconut milk, then pour over onions and cucumber and simmer gently for 6 minutes. Add vegetables and beanshoorts and simmer for 2 minutes, stirring often.

Serve with freshly fried krupuk.

SPICY FRUIT SALAD

RUJAK MANIS

Though this dish is called a fruit salad it is made up of a mixture of fresh fruits and vegetables (any crisp ones will do). The pungent, spicy sauce makes this salad a perfect accompaniment to other main dishes.

3 teaspoons tamarind
½ cup boiling water
3½ tablespoons sweet soya sauce
½ teaspoon dried shrimp paste
salt
3 fresh red chillies, sliced
375 g (¾ lb) peeled mixed fruit and vegetables
(cucumber, green pear, unripe mango, pineapple,
onion, apple, *salak,* partially cooked green beans)

Prepare vegetables and fruit by washing, peeling and slicing thinly. Soak tamarind in boiling water, then strain, reserving liquid. Mix tamarind water with sweet

Indonesian Vegetable Salad (recipe page 34).

soya sauce, shrimp paste and a pinch of salt. Pour into a small saucepan and simmer for 2 minutes. Cool.

Arrange vegetables and fruit in a serving dish or salad bowl. Scatter on sliced chillies and pour on the sauce. Serve slightly chilled.

INDONESIAN VEGETABLE SALAD

GADO GADO

Sauce: (prepare first)
1 medium onion, minced
2 cloves garlic, minced
155 g (5 oz) roasted peanuts, crushed
2 teaspoons dark soya sauce
1 tablespoon brown sugar
2 heaped teaspoons chilli powder
½ teaspoon salt
1 teaspoon tamarind
3 *daun salam* or bay leaves (optional)
3 tablespoons coconut or vegetable oil
¾ cup thick coconut milk
1 fresh red chilli, finely chopped

Fry all ingredients from onion to *daun salam* or bay leaves in the coconut or vegetable oil for 5 minutes, stirring frequently. Add coconut milk and simmer until sauce is thick and aromatic. Add chilli and leave to cool.

Salad:
2 small carrots
2 medium potatoes
100 g (3½ oz) cabbage, shredded
155 g (5 oz) green beans, sliced
250 g (½ lb) beanshoots
12 lettuce leaves
2 medium tomatoes
3 hardboiled eggs
1 small cucumber
freshly fried *krupuk*
dry fried onion flakes (this page)

Scrape carrots and slice thinly, or grate. Peel potatoes and cut into 1 cm (½ inch) dice or thin slices. Drop into boiling, slightly salted water and cook for 10 minutes. Add carrot and cook for 1 more minute. Drain and set aside. Saute cabbage and beans in a very little oil and water until partially cooked but still crisp. Put beanshoots in a strainer and pour on boiling water, or steep in a pot of boiling water for 2 minutes to soften. Drain. Wash lettuce and dry carefully.

Line a wide plate with the lettuce, top with carrot and potato pieces, then add beans and cabbage. Stack beanshoots on top. Cut tomatoes into thin wedges. Peel and slice cucumber. Slice boiled eggs. Arrange tomato, cucumber and egg slices attractively around the edge of the salad.

Pour on sauce and sprinkle with onion flakes. Decorate with freshly fried *krupuk*. Serve slightly chilled.

FRESH TOMATO SAMBAL

2 ripe tomatoes, skinned and chopped
1 small onion, finely chopped

½ red chilli, chopped
1 teaspoon salt
½ teaspoon dried shrimp paste, toasted
3 teaspoons water

Mix all ingredients together and pound in a mortar or puree in a blender until smooth. Store in an airtight jar in the refrigerator. This *sambal* will keep for up to 3 days.

If preferred do not pound the *sambal* but serve the ingredients finely chopped.

SHRIMP PASTE SAMBAL

SAMBAL TERASI

1 tablespoon dried shrimp paste, toasted
1 fresh red chilli, finely chopped
1 small onion
1-2 teaspoons sugar
1½ tablespoons oil
lemon or lime juice

Mash shrimp paste and mix with chilli. Mince onion and fry with sugar for 2 minutes. Add to shrimp paste and stir. Add lemon juice to taste.

This *sambal* may be kept in a sealed jar for up to 2 weeks.

SOYA SAUCE SAMBAL

2 tablespoons dark soya sauce
1 clove garlic, crushed
1 teaspoon sugar
½ fresh red chilli, finely chopped

Pour soya sauce into a bowl. Pound garlic, sugar and chilli to a paste and add to the sauce. Stir until sugar dissolves, then leave for 1 hour before using.

DRY FRIED ONION FLAKES

small red onions or shallots

Peel onions and slice as thinly as possible. Pat with kitchen paper to absorb excess moisture.

Heat a heavy-based frying pan and wipe out with an oiled cloth. Turn heat to moderate and put in onion. Cook uncovered until the onion is deeply coloured and dry underneath. Turn and cook other side. Ensure that the onion is completely dried out by placing in a warm oven for ½ hour. Store in an airtight container.

This is a very slow process and the cooking should not be accelerated or the onions will burn and become bitter. Make large amounts at a time and store until needed. If onions become slightly soft after storage, they can be crisped by placing in a warm oven for a few minutes.

SWEET CORN FRITTERS

BREGEDEL JAGUNG

440 g (14 oz) can whole kernel sweet corn

5 spring onions
2 cloves garlic
salt
pepper
2 eggs
75 g (2½ oz) plain flour
1½ teaspoons baking powder
100 g (3½ oz) cooked shrimps, chopped (optional)
2 tablespoons celery, finely chopped
oil for deep frying

Drain corn and crush lightly. Mince spring onions and garlic and mix with corn, salt and pepper.

Beat eggs lightly. Sift on flour and baking powder and stir in corn mixture, shrimps and celery. Stir thoroughly with a wooden spoon until batter is well mixed.

Heat oil in a shallow pan and drop in heaped teaspoonsful of the batter, several at a time. Cook to a deep golden brown.

Lift out and drain on absorbent paper. Serve hot or cold.

PEANUT CRISPS

REMPEYEK

Makes 30.

155 g (5 oz) peanuts
100 g (3½ oz) rice flour
2 tablespoons cornflour
⅓ cup warm water, or more
1 small onion
2 cloves garlic
3 teaspoons salt
2 teaspoons coriander, ground
1 heaped teaspoon chilli powder
½ cup boiling water
oil for deep frying

Roast peanuts, rub skins off and crush lightly. Mix rice flour, cornflour and warm water. Chop onion and garlic finely and add to the batter. Season with salt, coriander and chilli powder. Beat well, then pour in boiling water and beat to a smooth batter. Stand for 10 minutes. Stir in roasted peanuts and blend thoroughly.

Heat oil to smoking point in a shallow pan. Drop in a tablespoonful of the mixture and cook to a golden brown to test consistency of batter. Remove from oil and drain well. The cooked crisp should have a light, lacy appearance. If not, add a little more liquid to the batter, and cook the remaining crisps.

BANANA FRITTERS

PISANG GORENG

2 tablespoons sugar
2 eggs
100 g (3½ oz) plain flour
½ cup water
4 large bananas, ripe but firm
oil for deep frying

Beat sugar and eggs and blend in flour and enough water to form a smooth batter, not too thick. Beat thoroughly then let stand for 20 minutes.

Slice bananas diagonally. Coat lightly with batter and fry in hot oil until golden brown. Lift out and drain on absorbent paper. Serve hot or cold.

Pieces of pineapple, jackfruit or apple may also be prepared in this way. For variety, roll fritters in toasted coconut or serve with hot sugar syrup.

COCONUT CUSTARD WITH RICE

SERIKAYA KETAN

315 g (10 oz) glutinous rice
2¼ cups thin coconut milk
½ cup water
6 eggs
¾ cup thick coconut milk
1 tablespoon brown sugar
1 teaspoon salt
125 g (¼ lb) palm sugar or brown sugar
water

Wash rice, drain and put into a saucepan with thin coconut milk and water. Bring to the boil, cover, turn heat down and simmer until rice is tender.

Beat eggs lightly and stir in thick coconut milk, sugar and salt. Pour rice pudding into a 1¾ litre capacity (about 3 pints) ovenproof dish and top with the egg and coconut milk batter. Steam over a saucepan of boiling water, or cook in a moderate oven (180°C/350°F/Gas Mark 4) standing the dish in a tray of water. Cook until firm.

Allow to cool then chill well. Serve with sugar syrup made by boiling palm sugar or brown sugar together with water.

BANANA CAKES

Makes 24.

5 large bananas
100 g (3½ oz) coloured green pea flour *(tepong hoen kwe)* or substitute arrowroot and green food colouring
75 g (2½ oz) sugar, or to taste
pinch of salt
2½ cups thin coconut milk
1½ cups water
banana leaf or aluminium foil

Steam bananas in their skins for about 10 minutes until soft. Set aside to cool, then slice.

Put flour, sugar, and salt into a saucepan and add coconut milk and water. Bring to the boil, stirring continually, and simmer until the paste turns thick and begins to clear.

Cut banana leaf or foil into 15 cm (6 inch) squares and place a spoonful of the mixture on each. Add a slice of banana and top with a little more batter. Fold leaf or foil around the mixture to make a square shape. Tie with cotton or secure with toothpicks. Set aside to cool, then place in the refrigerator until set completely.

Serve wrapped or with the wrapper torn away at the top.

THAILAND

PORK AND MUSHROOM SOUP WITH SHRIMPS

KAENG KUNG KAP HET

2 tablespoons oil or butter
2 cloves garlic, crushed
½ teaspoon white pepper
½ teaspoon coriander, ground
½ teaspoon cummin, ground
½ teaspoon chilli powder
1 bay leaf
3 teaspoons fish sauce
125 g (¼ lb) sliced roast pork *(cha siu)*
1½ teaspoons salt
6 cups beef or chicken stock
100 g (3½ oz) peeled shrimp, precooked
100 g (3½ oz) canned straw mushrooms or champignons, drained
fresh coriander leaves, chopped

Heat oil or butter and fry crushed garlic with pepper, coriander, cummin, chilli powder and bay leaf for 2 minutes. Add fish sauce, roast pork and salt. Stir for 2 minutes on moderate heat, then pour in stock and bring to the boil. Turn heat down and simmer for 10 minutes. Add shrimp and mushrooms and cook for a further 6 minutes.
Garnish with chopped coriander before serving.

SOUR PRAWN SOUP

TOM YAM KUNG

6 cups fish or chicken stock
1 lemon or lime
4 lemon or lime leaves (or one lemon rind)
2 stalks lemon grass, each cut into 4 pieces
2 cloves garlic, crushed
2 fresh red chillies, finely chopped
1 tablespoon fish sauce
2 teaspoons coriander, ground
3 teaspoons chilli powder (or to taste)
2 teaspoons salt
½ teaspoon white pepper
¼ teaspoon monosodium glutamate (optional)
750 g (1½ lb) medium prawns
lemon or lime juice
6 spring onions, finely chopped

Slice lemon or lime into quarters. Combine all ingredients except prawns, lemon or lime juice and spring onions in a charcoal boiler or a large saucepan and bring to a rapid boil. Cook for 10 minutes on moderate heat then take to the table, bring to the boil again and cook for a further 10 minutes.
Add whole prawns, unpeeled, and cook for 7 minutes. Squeeze in lemon or lime juice to taste and garnish with spring onions.

BUTTERED FISH

SOON TIM YEE

375 g (¾ lb) fish fillets (cod, whiting, beam)
1 teaspoon salt
¼ teaspoon white pepper
cornflour
185 g (6 oz) butter
½ cucumber, peeled
2 tomatoes
60 g (2 oz) canned bamboo shoots, drained
2 slices pineapple
2.5 cm (1 inch) piece fresh ginger, shredded
1 small onion, minced
1 fresh red chilli, finely chopped
½ teaspoon coriander, ground
1 clove garlic, crushed
½ cup water or fish stock
1 teaspoon sugar
2 teaspoons fish sauce or light soya sauce
fresh coriander leaves, chopped
lemon slices

Slice fish fillets thinly. Season with salt and pepper, then coat very lightly with cornflour. Heat butter and fry fish on moderate heat for 2 minutes on each side. Drain and set aside, leaving butter in pan.
Cut vegetables into thin slices and soak cucumber and bamboo shoots in cold water. Cut pineapple into small wedges.
Add ginger, onion, chilli, coriander and garlic to the pan and saute for 2 minutes. Drain vegetables, add to pan, and saute for 4 minutes, stirring constantly. Pour in stock or water and season with sugar and fish or soya sauce. Simmer for 3-4 minutes, stirring occasionally. Season to taste with salt and pepper.
Return fish to the pan and reheat. Lift onto a warmed serving dish and cover with the vegetables, pineapple and sauce. Garnish with shredded coriander and surround with lemon slices.

MARINATED FISH

6 small fillets of whiting, trout or sole
3 tablespoons lime juice
2 tablespoons fish sauce or light soya sauce
⅔ cup thin coconut milk
2 spring onions
1 green chilli
lettuce leaves

Cut fish fillets into thin strips and place in a bowl. Cover with a marinade of lime juice, fish sauce or soya sauce and coconut milk. Cover dish with plastic film and stand for 24 hours in a cool place.
Shred spring onions and chilli. Drain fish. Arrange lettuce leaves in six glass cocktail bowls and top with a serving of the fish. Garnish with shredded chilli sauce

Pork-stuffed Oranges (recipe page 40).

and spring onion. A little more lime juice may be sprinkled on before serving.

Alternatively, line a serving dish with lettuce, arrange fish on top, garnish with the onion and chilli and pour marinade over the dish.

FISH FRIED WITH GINGER SAUCE
PLA PRIU WAN LHING

Pla Kapong is a fish caught in the klongs *(water canals) which run through Bangkok and across much of the Thai countryside. Bream or snapper make a good substitute for this meaty fish.*

Pla Kapong fish, weighing about 625 g (1¼ lb)
2 tablespoons oil
1 teaspoon salt
2 tablespoons cornflour
oil for frying

Sauce:
2 tablespoons white vinegar
5 cm (2 inch) piece fresh ginger, shredded
2 tablespoons sugar
1 teaspoon salt
¼ teaspoon monosodium glutamate (optional)
½ cup water
1 fresh red chilli, finely chopped
4 spring onions, finely chopped
1 tablespoon oil
cornflour
pickled ginger
cucumber slices

Clean fish and wash inside and out. Dry thoroughly. Rub with oil and salt, then coat with cornflour.

Heat about 5 cm (2 inches) oil in a *wok* or frying pan and fry fish, turning once or twice, until golden brown and slightly crisp. Test with a skewer in the thickest part to see if fish is cooked through. When done, lift out and keep warm.

Mix vinegar with ginger, sugar, salt and monosodium glutamate (if used). Stir in water and bring to the boil in a small saucepan. Simmer on moderate heat for 4-5 minutes.

Saute red chilli and spring onions in oil and add to the sauce. Thicken with a little cornflour mixed with cold water and stir sauce until it clears and thickens.

Put fish on an oblong serving plate and pour on the piping hot sauce. Garnish with pickled ginger and cucumber.

PRAWNS IN SPICED COCONUT SAUCE

12 large raw prawns
1 large onion
2 tablespoons oil
2 stalks lemon grass, chopped
2 fresh red or green chillies, sliced
2.5 (1 inch) piece fresh ginger, shredded
2 tablespoons fish sauce or light soya sauce
1 cup thick coconut milk
2 medium tomatoes, peeled and chopped

1 teaspoon sugar
½ teaspoon white pepper

Remove shells from prawns, leaving tails and heads intact. Remove dark veins and slit prawns down the underside from the head to tail.

Chop onion finely and fry in oil until soft. Add lemon grass, sliced chillies and ginger and saute for 2 minutes, then add fish sauce or soya sauce with coconut milk. Add tomatoes to the pan, with a little water. Cook on low heat until tomato is soft and sauce well flavoured.

Add prawns and simmer for about 5 minutes till tender. Season with sugar and white pepper.

MUSSELS WITH THAI HERBS
HOY MANGPOO OB MOR DIN

4 dozen fresh mussels, cleaned and scraped
6 cups water
6 lemon or lime leaves
1 lemon rind
2 stalks lemon grass
1 tablespoon salt
3 fresh red chillies, sliced
3 spring onions, chopped

Bring water to the boil in a deep pot. Add lemon leaves, rind, lemon grass and salt. Put in mussels, cover pot and bring to the boil. Cook, shaking pot from time to time, until mussels open. Drain, reserving half the stock. Put mussels in a deep serving dish, discarding ones which have not opened.

Strain reserved stock, discarding leaves, rind and lemon grass. Bring to the boil. Add chilli and spring onions and boil for 2 minutes. Pour over mussels and serve immediately.

SPICED OYSTERS
YAM HOY NANG LOM

4 dozen very small or 2 dozen medium sized oysters
2 tablespoons oil
8 spring onions or 6 shallots, finely chopped
4 cloves garlic, minced
2.5 cm (1 inch) piece fresh ginger, minced
3 teaspoons dried shrimp paste
90 g (3 oz) salted fish, soaked and ground
2 tablespoons sugar, or to taste
2 teaspoons fish sauce or light soya sauce
½ teaspoon white pepper
1½ teaspoons chilli powder
1 heaped tablespoon chopped fresh coriander leaves
¾ cup water
lemon juice
lemon wedges

Heat oil and saute onion, garlic and ginger for 3 minutes. Mix shrimp paste with ground salted fish, sugar, fish or soya sauce, pepper, and chilli powder. Add to the pan and saute for 2 minutes. Stir in chopped coriander leaves and water, then simmer on moderate heat for 2 minutes. Add oysters and cook for 5 minutes. Thicken sauce with a little cornflour, if necessary.

Spoon into a serving dish and sprinkle on lemon juice to taste. Surround with lemon wedges.

CRABMEAT AND PORK ROLLS
PRATAT LOM

185 g (6 oz) fresh crab meat
250 g (½ lb) pork shoulder or leg
75 g (2½ oz) canned bamboo shoots, drained
10 dried black mushrooms, soaked
2 tablespoons vegetable oil
2 cloves garlic, finely chopped
1½ teaspoons salt
½ teaspoon white pepper
2 teaspoons coriander, ground
½ tablespoon fish sauce, or light soya sauce
2 teaspoons cornflour
2 dozen frozen spring roll wrappers, or rice paper
    wrappers
oil for deep frying

Sauce:
3 tablespoons fish sauce or light soya sauce
1 tablespoon white vinegar
3 green chillies

Shred crab meat. Finely mince or dice pork. Slice bamboo shoots and black mushrooms into thin threads.

Heat oil and fry minced pork with garlic until cooked through. Add bamboo shoots and mushrooms, frying on moderate heat for 5 minutes before adding shredded crabmeat. Season with salt, white pepper, coriander and fish sauce or soya sauce. Remove from heat, sprinkle on cornflour and stir well. Allow to cool thoroughly before preparing rolls.

Place a spoonful of the filling on each wrapper and roll up, turning ends in securely. Well the outside edge with water and stick doen firmly. Heat oil to smoking point and drop in rolls, several at a time. Cook quickly to a light golden brown, then lift out and drain.

To prepare sauce, slice chillies and mix with other ingredients. Pour into several small bowls and serve with the fried rolls.

FRIED CHICKEN WITH SWEET BASIL AND CHILLI

315 g (10 oz) chicken breast
60 g (2 oz) chicken liver and giblets (optional)
2 tablespoons vegetable oil
4 tablespoons very small green birds-eye chillies or
    6 green chillies, sliced
1 small bunch fresh sweet basil leaves
2 tablespoons parsley, finely chopped
2 tablespoons fish sauce

Chop chicken breast, liver and giblets into very small dice. Heat oil and fry chicken on moderate heat for 3 minutes, then add chillies, half the basil and the chopped parsley. Cook, stirring frequently, for 5 minutes. Splash on fish sauce and stir briefly.

Spoon chicken and herbs onto a serving dish and surround with remaining sweet basil leaves.

CHICKEN IN PEANUT AND COCONUT SAUCE
KAI PENANG

1.5 kg (3 lb) chicken
2 teaspoons salt
½ teaspoon white pepper
2 cloves garlic, crushed
1½ cups thick coconut milk
2 tablespoons cummin seeds, ground
1 tablespoon coriander, ground
3 teaspoons light soya sauce
3 fresh red chillies, finely chopped
2 teaspoons sugar
1 teaspoon dried shrimp paste
2 heaped tablespoons roasted peanuts, coarsely ground
lemon or lime juice
fresh coriander leaves, chopped
fresh red chilli, shredded

Clean chicken and wipe dry. Rub with salt, pepper and crushed garlic. Put in a deep pot and pour on coconut milk. Cover and simmer on low heat for 1 hour. Lift out chicken, cool and cut into bite-sized pieces. Set aside, keeping warm.

Reheat sauce and add all remaining ingredients except lemon or lime juice and garnish. Simmer for 2 minutes. Return chicken and cook until chicken is very tender.

Arrange chicken pieces on a serving dish, sprinkle with lemon or lime juice and pour on sauce. Garnish with chopped coriander leaves and shredded red chilli.

BEEF WITH VEGETABLES IN OYSTER SAUCE
SUB GUM NGOU YUK

250 g (½ lb) lean topside, sirloin or rump steak
¾ teaspoon salt
90 g (3 oz) green beans
1 large green pepper
3 medium tomatoes
75 g (2½ oz) canned bamboo shoots, drained
3 tablespoons oil
1 tablespoon dark soya sauce
2 tablespoons oyster sauce
2 teaspoons sugar
1 cup beef stock
1 teaspoon cornflour
fresh coriander leaves, chopped
spring onions, shredded

Slice beef into pieces about 5 cm (2 inches) square and 1 cm (½ inch) thick. Season with salt.

Cut beans into 5 cm (2 inch) pieces. Wipe peppers, remove seeds and stems and cut into 2.5 cm (1 inch) squares. Quarter tomatoes, removing seeds. Slice bamboo shoots thinly.

Heat oil and brown meat well. Add vegetables and soya sauce and saute for 3 minutes, stirring frequently. Pour on oyster sauce, sugar and stock, cover and cook on moderate heat for 5 minutes, stirring from time to time.

Mix cornflour with a little cold water and stir into the sauce. Cook until sauce thickens and clears. Lift meat slices from the sauce and arrange on a serving dish. Surround with vegetables and pour on sauce. Garnish with chopped coriander and shredded spring onion.

BEEF AND WATER CHESTNUTS

PRA RAM LONG SONG

375 g (¾ lb) round, topside or knuckle beef
2 tablespoons oil
6 cloves garlic, crushed
10 shallots or 3 small red onions, sliced
1 teaspoon coriander seeds
2 cups thin coconut milk
2 teaspoons dried shrimp paste
1 teaspoon sugar
5 dried chillies, crushed
10 cm (4 inch) stalk lemon grass, chopped
125 g (¼ lb) roasted peanuts, crushed
salt
pepper
220 g (7 oz) canned water chestnuts, drained and sliced
½ cup thick coconut milk
fresh coriander or mint sprigs

Slice beef and cut into 5 cm (2 inch) squares.

Heat oil and fry garlic, onions and coriander for 2 minutes. Push to the side of the pan and fry beef slices until well browned. Pour in thin coconut milk and add shrimp paste, sugar, chillies, lemon grass and peanuts. Mix well and bring almost to the boil. Turn heat down and simmer for 10-12 minutes. Season to taste with salt and pepper and keep warm.

Boil sliced water chestnuts in slightly salted water for 2 minutes, then drain and add to the curry with thick coconut milk. Heat through, then spoon into a serving dish. Garnish with coriander or mint.

PORK OMELETTE

RUM

Makes 1 serving.

1½ tablespoons vegetable oil
1 clove garlic, minced
60 g (2 oz) lean pork, minced
3 teaspoons light soya sauce
monosodium glutamate (optional)
6 slices green chilli
2 eggs
spring onion, chopped
salt
pepper
fresh coriander sprigs
tomato and cucumber slices

Heat oil in a small saucepan and fry garlic for 1 minute. Add minced pork and saute on moderate heat until browned. Season with soya sauce and monosodium glutamate (if used) and stir in chilli slices. Remove from heat.

Beat eggs lightly and pour into lightly oiled omelette pan. Cook on moderate heat until egg begins to set. Spread minced pork and chopped spring onions over the omelette. Season to taste with salt and pepper and cook for a further minute.

Roll up and lift onto a heated plate. Garnish with a sprig or two of coriander and surround with tomato and cucumber slices.

PORK-STUFFED ORANGES

MA HOU

6 large oranges
1½ tablespoons oil
8 cloves garlic, minced
6 spring onions, finely chopped
1-2 fresh red chillies, chopped
1 heaped tablespoon roasted peanuts, crushed
625 g (1¼ lb) lean pork, minced
1 teaspoon dried shrimp paste
2 teaspoons light soya sauce
1½ teaspoons coriander, ground
1½ teaspoons salt
½ teaspoon white pepper
1 teaspoon sugar
oil
6 sprigs of mint

Cut oranges in half and scoop out most of the flesh, leaving a 1 cm (½ inch) layer attached to the skin.

Heat oil and saute garlic and spring onion for 2 minutes. Add chilli and peanuts and cook for a further 2 minutes, stirring frequently. Stir in minced pork, shrimp paste, soya sauce, coriander, salt, pepper and sugar. Cook, stirring occasionally, on moderate heat until meat is cooked through.

Stuff mixture into oranges, pressing in firmly. Round off tops and place oranges in a large baking pan or oven-proof tray. Brush with a little oil. Bake in a pre-heated moderate oven (180°C/350°F/Gas Mark 4) for 15 minutes, brushing with a little more oil during cooking.

Serve two orange halves on each plate, decorating each pair with a sprig of mint.

THAI RICE

500 g (1 lb) long grain rice
1 large onion
1 fresh red chilli
3 tablespoons oil
2.5 cm (1 inch) piece fresh ginger, minced
1 *pandan* leaf (optional), or
    4 curry leaves
5 cm (2 inch) stick cinnamon
2 teaspoons salt
5½ cups thin coconut milk
fresh red and green chilli
fried dried fish (optional)

Wash rice in cold water, drain and allow to dry for about ½ hour. Mince onion and chilli. Pour rice into a large heavy-based saucepan and pour in oil. Stir on high heat for 2 minutes until rice grains are thoroughly

Coconut Pancakes (recipe page 43).

coated. Stir in remaining ingredients except fresh chillies and dried fish.

Cover saucepan tightly and cook on very low heat for about 15 minutes, until all liquid is absorbed into the rice and each grain is soft and tender. Discard *pandan* or curry leaves and cinnamon stick.

Spoon rice into a deep serving dish. Garnish with shredded red and green chilli and threads of fried dried fish, if available.

FRIED THAI NOODLES

MEE KROB

4 Chinese dried mushrooms, soaked in cold water for ½ hour
155 g (5 oz) chicken meat
60 g (2 oz) chicken livers
75 g (2½ oz) Chinese roast pork (*cha siu*)
60 g (2 oz) cabbage or Chinese cabbage
2 squares hard beancurd (optional)
60 g (2 oz) canned bamboo shoots
vegetable oil
1 kg (2 lb) fresh Chinese egg noodles, parboiled
1 cm (½ inch) piece fresh ginger, minced
2 cloves garlic, crushed
6 spring onions, chopped
2 fresh red chillies, thinly sliced
60 g (2 oz) beanshoots
75 g (2½ oz) raw shrimp, peeled
1 tablespoon fish sauce
1½ teaspoons chilli powder
1 teaspoon salt
¼ teaspoon monosodium glutamate (optional)
½ cup chicken stock
2 teaspoons cornflour

Chop chicken, livers and pork into 1 cm (½ inch) dice. Wash and chop cabbage, shake out water. Cut beancurd into 0.5 cm (¼ inch) dice. Drain bamboo shoots and slice thinly.

Heat 2 tablespoons oil and stir-fry noodles for 3-4 minutes, then remove to a warmed plate. Add ginger and garlic to the pan and cook 1 minute. Add spring onions, sliced chillies, beanshoots and shrimp and saute for 2 minutes. Remove and keep warm. Heat a little more oil and saute cabbage, bamboo shoots and beancurd for 2 minutes.

In another pan, fry meat until lightly coloured, then season with fish sauce, chilli powder, salt and monosodium glutamate (if used). Pour on stock, bring to the boil and cook for 5 minutes, until meat is tender. Thicken gravy with cornflour mixed with a little cold water. Pour meat over vegetables, adding beanshoots and shrimp. Mix well then spoon over noodles.

Serve with Chinese brown vinegar or chopped chilli mixed with soya sauce.

GREEN PAPAYA SALAD

250 g (½ lb) hard green papaya (pawpaw)
125 g (¼ lb) green beans
2 medium tomatoes
¼ cup thick coconut milk
2 tablespoons fish sauce or light soya sauce
2 cloves garlic, crushed
2 tablespoons roasted peanuts, crushed

Peel papaya and grate. Cover with cold water. Remove strings from beans and cut into 2.5 cm (1 inch) lengths. Cook in slightly salted water until done, but still crisp. Drain and refresh with cold water. Put tomatoes into boiling water, count to seven, then lift out and peel. Cut into thin wedges. Drain papaya.

Arrange papaya, beans and tomato wedges in a salad bowl. mix coconut milk with fish sauce or soya sauce and stir in crushed garlic. Pour onto the salad and toss a little.

Sprinkle on crushed peanuts. Garnish, if desired, with sprigs of fresh coriander.

STUFFED EGGPLANT

KAYANTHI HNAT

1 dozen very small eggplants
salt
250 g (½ lb) raw shrimp, peeled
185 g (6 oz) chicken breast
1 medium onion
4 cloves garlic
1 tablespoon chilli powder
1 teaspoon turmeric powder
1 tablespoon parsley or chopped fresh coriander leaves
oil for deep frying
1 egg
3 tablespoons cornflour
3 tablespoons plain flour

Wipe eggplants and cut off tops. Scoop out centres and chop into small dice. Season with a little salt and set aside. Fill eggplants with salted water and stand for 3-4 minutes.

Chop shrimp and chicken into small dice and finely chop onions and garlic. Add chopped eggplants and season with chilli powder, turmeric and chopped parsley or coriander. Bind with 2 tablespoons oil and stir in 1½ teaspoons salt. Knead to a smooth paste. Drain eggplants, wipe out and stuff with the meat filling.

Make a thick batter with the egg, cornflour and flour, adding a little salt and cold water. Beat till smooth.

Heat oil and when at smoking point, lower heat slightly. Coat eggplant with the batter and drop into the oil, several pieces at a time. Cook for about 7 minutes, lift out and cool slightly.

Just before serving return to hot oil for a further 3 minutes. Drain and serve hot.

THREE KINDS OF CHICKEN

The origin of this unusual and totally unrelated name remains a mystery.

2 tablespoons roasted peanuts
sliced spring onions
1 lemon or lime
1½ tablespoons dried shrimps
4 cm (1½ inch) piece fresh ginger
1 tablespoon birds-eye chillies
10 cm (4 inch) stalk lemon grass, chopped

Cut lime or lemon into thin slices, then into tiny pieces. Slice ginger. Arrange all ingredients in separate piles on a serving platter or in small bowls on a tray.

Serve as an appetiser, or as nibblers with drinks.

FISH SAUCE

NAM PLA

Nam Pla is a strongly flavoured salty fish sauce produced by fermentation of dried fish. It is used constantly in Thai food in the same way that soya sauce is used in Chinese cooking — to add flavour and a salty taste to dishes. Vietnamese nuoc mam is a similar sauce, as is the salty fish sauce labelled 'Fish Gravy' available in the West. If Fish Gravy is not available, the following recipe produces a good substitute. It can be prepared in advance for convenience, and kept for several weeks in a sealed container without loss of flavour.

12 anchovy fillets, or
   4 tablespoons salted anchovy essence
1-2 teaspoons sugar
2 tablespoon light soya sauce

Pound anchovy fillets to a smooth paste. Add a little water, then blend in sugar and soya sauce. Blend in a liquidiser to make a smooth sauce. Pour into a jar and seal tightly.

THAI HOT SAUCE

NAM PRIK

Some dishes served in Thailand are of a relatively mild flavour and are served with tasty hot sauces similar to the sambals of Malaysia and Indonesia. This particular sauce goes well with meat, vegetable, noodle or rice dishes and is a good standby. It can be prepared up to 2 weeks in advance and improves in flavour after standing for several days.

2 tablespoons dried shrimps, soaked
3 teaspoons salt
1 teaspoon brown sugar
4 cloves garlic
6 anchovy fillets, or 1 tablespoon salted anchovy essence
1 tablespoon light soya sauce
4-5 fresh red chillies
lemon or lime juice

Pound all ingredients, except lemon or lime juice, to a smooth paste. Sprinkle on juice to taste and stir into the sauce. Spoon into a jar and seal tightly.

FRIED COCONUT CAKES

MOK SI KAO

100 g (3½ oz) palm sugar or brown sugar
3 cups water
250 g (½ lb) rice flour
1 egg
2 teaspoons baking powder
pinch of salt
125 g (¼ lb) grated fresh coconut or desiccated coconut
oil for deep frying

Dissolve sugar in water over moderate heat. Leave to cool. Make a paste of rice flour, egg, baking powder, salt and coconut. Pour in syrup and beat to make a smooth batter. Leave for 20 minutes.

Heat oil to smoking point, then lower heat and drop in large spoonfuls of the batter. Fry to a deep golden colour. Remove and drain well. Cool before serving.

Sliced banana, apple, jackfruit or pineapple may be added to the batter.

COCONUT PANCAKES

KHAN UM KLUK

2½ cups thin coconut milk
100 g (3½ oz) rice flour
3 eggs
125 g (¼ lb) sugar
90 g (3 oz) desiccated coconut
green and pink food colouring
pinch of salt
oil
¼ cup desiccated or grated coconut

Make a thin batter with coconut milk, rice flour, eggs and sugar. Beat for 5 minutes, then fold in 90 g desiccated coconut. Divide the batter into three portions. Colour one pink, one bright green and leave one plain. Add a little salt to each and beat well. Leave for at least 20 minutes.

Wipe a 15 cm (6 inch) omelette pan with an oiled cloth and heat through. When ready, pour in a thin layer of batter and swirl pan to thinly cover the bottom. Cook pancake on moderate heat until flecked with brown underneath. Flip over and cook other side. Roll up in the pan and slide onto a plate. Cook all pancakes and stack the different colours in groups on a serving plate.

Garnish with desiccated or grated coconut and serve warm or cold.

THE PHILIPPINES

PRAWNS IN VEGETABLE SOUP

SINIGANG NA SUGPO

6 raw tiger prawns, or 12 raw king prawns
7 cups water
1½ tablespoons tamarind, or
   juice of 2 lemons or limes
⅓ cup hot water
2 large tomatoes, quartered
185 g (6 oz) green beans, sliced
185 g (6 oz) cabbage, chopped
1 teaspoon white pepper
salt

Boil prawns in water for 10 minutes. Remove prawns on a slotted spoon and return stock to the heat to reduce to 4½ cups.

Soak tamarind in hot water for 15 minutes. Strain tamarind water or lemon or lime juice into the pot and add all vegetables. Bring to the boil and cook until tender.

Return prawns and season with pepper. Add salt to taste, and cook for another minute.

Chilli sauce, soya sauce or additional lemon or lime juice may be added, to taste.

PRAWNS ADOBO

ADOBONG SUGPO

375 g (¾ lb) large raw prawns
2 cloves garlic, finely chopped
2½ tablespoons white vinegar
½ teaspoon black pepper
1 teaspoon salt
1 bay leaf
¾ cup water
3 tablespoons butter
1 rounded tablespoon plain flour
parsley, finely chopped

Peel and devein prawns, leaving heads and tails on. Mix garlic with vinegar, pepper, salt, bay leaf and water. Arrange prawns in a large saucepan and pour on the marinade. Cover and bring to the boil, then turn heat down and simmer for 3 minutes.

Lift out prawns with a slotted spoon and reduce sauce over high heat. Strain and set aside.

Melt 2 tablespoons of butter in a frying pan. Sprinkle on flour and stir over moderate heat until golden brown. Pour in strained liquid and beat briskly with a wire whisk until sauce is smooth and thick. Keep warm on low heat.

Melt remaining butter and fry prawns quickly on high heat, turning several times. Lift out and place on warmed serving dish. Coat with the sauce and garnish with parsley.

SOUR FISH WITH VEGETABLES

PAKSIW

500 g (1 lb) white fish fillets
1 tablespoon dried shrimps, soaked
75 g (2½ oz) canned or fresh bitter melon
1 small eggplant
2.5 cm (1 inch) piece fresh ginger
2-3 green chillies
¼ cup white wine vinegar
¾ cup fish stock or water
salt
1 teaspoon freshly ground black pepper

Cut fish into pieces about 6 cm (2½ inches) square. Drain shrimp, reserving liquid. Peel bitter melon and eggplant and cut into 2 cm (¾ inch) cubes. Slice ginger and green chillies thinly, removing seeds for milder flavour.

Put eggplant and bitter melon in a saucepan and arrange fish slices on top. Scatter on ginger and chilli and pour on vinegar, stock and shrimp liquid. Add salt and pepper and bring to the boil. Reduce heat and simmer until fish are tender.

Transfer to a serving dish and serve with rice or noodles.

CHICKEN ADOBO

1½ kg (3 lb) chicken
3 teaspoons salt
1 teaspoon black pepper
2 bay leaves
8-12 cloves garlic, crushed
¾ cup white vinegar
3 tablespoons oil

Clean chicken, rinse and wipe dry. Cut into large pieces and rub with salt and pepper. Put pieces into a deep saucepan and add bay leaves and crushed garlic. Pour on vinegar and marinate for 30 minutes.

Cook on moderate heat until chicken is tender, adding a little water or stock as liquid evaporates, to keep meat moist. When chicken is cooked, turn heat up for a few minutes to dry out any remaining liquid.

Pour oil into the pan and fry on high heat until chicken pieces are dark brown and crisp on the surface. Lift out and drain well before serving.

BAKED SPARE RIBS

1½ kg (3 lb) pork or beef spare ribs, trimmed
1 onion, quartered
2 tablespoons light soya sauce
½ teaspoon black pepper
2 teaspoons salt

Vegetable Salad Rolls (recipe page 46).

45

4 tablespoons oil
2 tablespoons sugar
2 tablespoons dark soya sauce

Sauce:
4 tablespoons brown sugar
1½ teaspoons salt
3 tablespoons dark soya sauce
1 large onion, minced
2 cm (¾ inch) piece fresh ginger, minced

Separate ribs. Put into a very large saucepan with onion, light soya sauce, pepper and salt. Cover with water and boil for 45 minutes. Preheat oven to 190°C/375°F/Gas Mark 5. Drain boiled ribs well and arrange in a lightly oiled baking pan.

Mix oil, sugar and dark soya sauce, stirring to dissolve sugar. Brush ribs with the mixture and bake until crisp and dark. Brush with more of the liquid during cooking.

To prepare sauce, mix all ingredients in a small saucepan. Add enough water to make a thin sauce and bring to the boil. Cook for 5 minutes, or until the sauce thickens slightly.

Serve in several small bowls or pour over the baked ribs before serving.

BARBECUED SUCKLING PIG WITH LIVER SAUCE

LECHON

6-7 kg (12-15 lb) suckling pig
12 bay leaves
salt
black pepper
750 g (1½ lb) melted lard
2½ cups boiling water

Liver Sauce:
1 pigs liver
1½ cups water
1 whole head of garlic
4 tablespoons lard
¼ medium onion, minced
30 g (1 oz) dried white breadcrumbs
30 g (1 oz) sugar
salt to taste
¼ cup white vinegar
1 teaspoon black pepper

Have the butcher clean and shave the pig. Wash it well and reserve the liver for the sauce. Put bay leaves inside the cavity after sprinkling inside with salt and pepper. Sew up opening or secure with toothpicks or metal pins.

Rub salt and pepper well into the skin. Brush the pig generously with melted lard, then pour on boiling water, allowing the oily liquid to run off into a metal drip tray or baking tin.

Cover the pig with greased paper and roast in a moderate oven (190°C/375°F/Gas Mark 5) for approximately 4½ hours. Lift paper and baste frequently with the pan juices during cooking. When almost done, remove paper and turn oven temperature up very high to slightly crisp the skin.

Suckling pig may be barbecued if preferred. Prepare as above and secure on a heavy metal rotisserie over a charcoal fire. Slowly turn over the coals until meat is done. It should be tender but still quite pink. Cooking time will depend on the heat of the fire and the size of the piglet, but it should be around 4 hours. Brush with melted lard at 15-minute intervals to prevent the skin becoming too dry.

To prepare the sauce, place the liver in a roasting pan and roast until quite brown on the outside. Push the liver through a fine wire sieve or mince finely. Pour on water and strain minced liver and water through a sieve. Discard any coarse pieces of liver or sinew.

Mince garlic and saute in lard until soft. Add onions, saute for 2 minutes, then stir in breadcrumbs, sugar, salt and vinegar. Stir well, then blend in the liver paste and season with pepper. Simmer on moderate heat, stirring continually until sauce becomes quite thick. Check seasonings. Pour into a sauce bowl.

Slice suckling pig into thin pieces and serve with the sauce.

VEGETABLE SALAD ROLLS

LUMPIA

Lumpia Wrappers:
315 (10 oz) plain flour
155 g (5 oz) rice flour
1 tablespoon salt
1 tablespoon oil
3 cups water
2 eggs

24 lettuce leaves

Lumpia Filling:
1 tablespoon oil
1 small onion, minced
4 cloves garlic, crushed
125 g (¼ lb) green beans, sliced
2 small carrots, grated
155 g (5 oz) cabbage, shredded finely
1 small sweet potatoes, peeled and grated, or
   90 g (3 oz) thinly sliced palm hearts
100 g (3½ oz) pork, finely diced
¼ cup water
90 g (3 oz) raw shrimps, peeled and finely diced
light soya sauce
salt and pepper

Sauce:
4 tablespoons brown sugar
1½ tablespoons cornflour
1½ tablespoons dark soya sauce
1 teaspoon salt
2 cups beef stock
4 cloves garlic

To prepare wrappers, sift flour, rice flour and salt into a bowl. Beat in oil, water and eggs and beat for 2 minutes. Leave to stand for 1 hour.

To prepare filling, heat oil and fry onion and garlic until soft. Add all vegetables and saute for 2 minutes.

Then add pork and stir on moderate heat for 6 minutes. Pour in water, cover and cook for 3 minutes.

Remove lid, add shrimps and season with soya sauce, salt and pepper to taste. Simmer, stirring, until liquid is evaporated and ingredients cooked through. Allow to cool before using.

To prepare the sauce, mix sugar, cornflour, soya sauce and salt in a small saucepan. Pour in stock and bring to a rapid boil. Cook over high heat, stirring frequently, until sauce thickens.

Peel and crush garlic and add to the sauce. Stir in and simmer for a further 2 minutes. Pour into one or two small sauce dishes.

To cook wrappers, heat a well oiled omelette pan and rub base with a paper towel. Pour in just enough prepared batter to thinly coat the pan. Swirl pan so it spreads as evenly as possible. Cook pancake on moderate heat until it can be easily lifted. Lift and turn. Cook other side to a light golden colour. Cook all batter and stack prepared pancakes between pieces of greaseproof paper.

Wash lettuce leaves and dry thoroughly.

To prepare the salad rolls, line each pancake with a lettuce leaf. Spoon on a generous amount of the filling and roll up. Serve with the sauce.

SAVOURY SHRIMP SNACKS

UKOY

100 g (3½ oz) raw baby shrimps, peeled
2½ cups water
155 g (5 oz) plain flour
1½ teaspoons salt
2 teaspoons baking powder
2 eggs, beaten
½-1 teaspoon white pepper
1 clove garlic, crushed
6 spring onions, finely chopped
oil for deep frying

Boil shrimps in water for 3 minutes. Drain, reserving ¾ cup liquid.

Sift flour, salt and baking powder into a bowl. Add beaten eggs and ½ cup of shrimp liquid and season with pepper, garlic and spring onions. Beat briskly. Chop shrimp and stir into the batter. Beat again. The batter should be of dropping consistency. If needed, add a little more of the reserved stock.

Heat oil to smoking point and drop spoonful of the batter into the hot oil. Lower heat slightly. Cook until the cakes rise to the surface, then cook for a further 2 minutes on moderate heat. Lift out and drain.

Serve with dips of vinegar, soya sauce or salt and pepper.

COCONUT RICE CAKE

BIBINGKA

¾ cup thick coconut milk
1 1/8 cups thin coconut milk
220 g (7 oz) rice flour
1 teaspoon salt
250 g (½ lb) brown sugar
¼ teaspoon anise or caraway seed, powdered

Mix ¼ cup thick coconut milk with thin coconut milk, rice flour and salt. Beat until batter is smooth. Cook in a double saucepan until batter is very thick, stirring frequently. Add a little more coconut milk if the mixture becomes too thick. Stir in all but 30 g (1 oz) sugar and beat well.

Grease a 23 cm (9 inch) baking tin and pour in the batter. Pour remaining thick coconut milk on top and sprinkle on remaining brown sugar and anise or caraway seed powder.

Cover with foil and bake in a moderate oven (180°C/350°F/Gas Mark 4) until firm. Cooking time is approximately 25 minutes.

Remove foil and cook until top is lightly browned, or place under a hot grill to brown top.

Serve either hot or cold.

BANANA ROLLS

3 medium very ripe bananas
6 Lumpia wrappers (see recipe page 46, using ¼ of mixture)
2 teaspoons white sesame seeds
2 tablespoons sugar
oil for deep frying

Syrup:
½ cup water
155 g (5 oz) sugar

Put bananas in a preheated moderate oven or under moderate grill and cook until tender (about 12 minutes). Turn frequently if cooking under grill.

Peel and cut into long, thin strips. Put several pieces on each Lumpia wrapper, sprinkle with sugar and sesame seeds and roll up, tucking ends in securely.

Heat oil to smoking point, lower heat slightly and deep fry until golden. Lift out and drain on absorbent paper.

Dissolve sugar in water and bring to the boil in a small saucepan. Simmer until syrup becomes slightly sticky.

Pour over fried banana rolls before serving, or serve in a separate dish to use as a dip. Banana Rolls may be served without the syrup or with a generous sprinkling of white sugar.

Note: Commercially prepared spring roll skins can be used instead of Lumpia wrappers.

MALAYSIA & SINGAPORE

FISH MOOLEE

750 g (1½ lb) cod, haddock or snapper
1 tablespoon tamarind
1¼ cups boiling water
2 cloves garlic
5 shallots
2 tablespoons oil
2.5 cm (1 inch) piece fresh ginger
1 stalk lemon grass
1 fresh red chilli, thinly sliced
½ teaspoon turmeric powder
1 teaspoon salt
¾ cup thin coconut milk
¾ cup thick coconut milk
fresh coriander leaves, chopped

Cut fish into fillets and remove skin. Cut fillets into pieces about 5 cm (2 inches) square. Soak tamarind in boiling water. Chop garlic and shallots finely. Shred ginger.

Heat oil in a pan and fry garlic and shallots for 2 minutes. Add ginger and cook for another minute. Add strained tamarind water with lemon grass, chilli, turmeric and salt. Bring to the boil, turn heat down and stir in thin coconut milk. When the sauce is almost boiling drop in fish slices and pour on thick coconut milk. Simmer for about 5 minutes until fish is tender.

Check seasonings, adding more salt if necessary. Spoon into a serving dish and garnish with chopped coriander leaves.

TAMARIND PRAWNS

UDANG ASAM

2 tablespoons tamarind
1 cup boiling water
500 g (1 lb) large raw prawns
2 teaspoons chilli powder
2 teaspoons sugar
2 tablespoons oil
185 g (6 oz) mixed pickled vegetables, or
   sliced tomato and cucumber

Soak tamarind in boiling water for 30 minutes. Remove shell from prawns, leaving heads and tails intact. Carefully scrape out dark veins with a sharp knife, then make deep incisions down the centre back of the prawns to make them curl up during cooking. Arrange prawns in a wide flat bowl. Strain tamarind water, and stir in chilli powder and sugar. Pour over prawns and marinate for up to 1 hour, turning occasionally.

Heat oil in a *wok* or large frying pan. Drain prawns and saute on high heat for 2 minutes. Pour on marinade and cook until prawns are tender. Remove prawns from sauce with a slotted spoon. Bring sauce to the boil and cook until well reduced.

Drain pickled vegetables and arrange these, or tomato and cucumber slices, around the edge of a serving dish. Place prawns in the centre and pour on the sauce.

SINGAPORE CHILLI CRAB

2 medium raw crabs
3 teaspoons tamarind
¾ cup boiling water
3 tablespoons oil
2 medium onions, minced
5 cm (2 inch) piece fresh ginger, minced
4 fresh red chillies, finely chopped
1-2 teaspoons chilli powder
2 teaspoons tomato paste
3 teaspoons sugar, or to taste
2 teaspoons cornflour
fresh red and green chillies, sliced
spring onions, chopped

Drop crabs into boiling, slightly salted water and cook rapidly for 4 minutes. Remove, drain and leave to cool. Soak tamarind in boiling water. Chop crabs into large pieces, if possible leaving the legs attached to the body pieces. Remove the spongey grey portion and discard.

Heat oil in a *wok* or very large pan and saute onion, ginger and chopped chillies for 2 minutes. Add crab pieces and sprinkle on chilli powder, then pour in strained tamarind water. Lower heat and simmer for 4 minutes.

Remove crab to a serving plate. Add tomato paste and sugar to the sauce. Thicken with cornflour mixed with a little cold water and cook until sauce thickens and clears slightly. Pour over crab.

Garnish with sliced chilli and spring onion.

ASSORTED SATAY

1 tablespoon coriander, ground
1 teaspoon fennel, ground (optional)
1½ teaspoons cummin, ground
3 cloves garlic, crushed
2-3 dried chillies, soaked
1 stalk lemon grass, chopped
2.5 cm (1 inch) piece fresh ginger, chopped
2 teaspoons sugar
1 teaspoon tamarind
1 teaspoon turmeric powder
1 kg (2 lb) beef, mutton, pork, chicken and raw
   prawns (mixed)
salt
¼ cup thick coconut milk
1½ tablespoons oil
36 bamboo skewers
2 large cucumbers

Satay Sauce:
2 teaspoons coriander, ground

Fried Rice Noodles (recipe page 52).

1 teaspoon cummin, ground
1 teaspoon fennel, ground
6 dried chillies, soaked
2 cloves garlic, chopped
3 shallots or 6 spring onions, chopped
1 heaped teaspoon dried shrimp paste
8 candlenuts
1 stalk lemon grass
1 tablespoon oil
155 g (5 oz) roasted peanuts, coarsely ground
¾ cup thick coconut milk
½ cup tamarind water, made with 2 teaspoons
   tamarind
sugar
salt

To prepare the Satay marinade, mix together coriander, fennel and cummin and roast briefly in a dry pan or under griller. Grind to a paste with garlic, chillies, lemon grass, ginger, sugar, tamarind and turmeric. Cut all meat into small thin pieces. Peel and devein prawns. Sprinkle with salt. Rub meat and prawns with the seasonings and stand for at least 1 hour to absorb flavours.

Prepare sauce. Grind coriander, cummin, fennel, chillies, garlic, shallots or spring onions, dried shrimp paste, candlenuts and lemon grass to a paste. Heat 1 tablespoon oil in pan and fry ground seasonings for 3 minutes. Add ground peanuts and stir in coconut milk slowly. Cook on moderate heat, stirring constantly, for 5 minutes.

Pour in tamarind water and add sugar and salt to taste. Bring almost to the boil, then turn heat down and simmer until oil begins to rise to the surface. Add a little more coconut milk or water if sauce becomes too thick.

Thread various types of meat and prawns onto separate bamboo skewers. Pour thick coconut milk and oil over the Satay and then place under a griller or over a charcoal fire to roast until done. The surface should be crisp and inside tender and juicy. Brush with a little more of the coconut milk and oil during cooking to prevent meat drying out.

Peel cucumbers or scrape with the prongs of a fork and rub with salt. Cut into 2.5 cm (1 inch) cubes and arrange on several plates. Serve cooked Satay with flat plates of sauce and the cucumber.

MALACCAN DEVIL'S CURRY

750 g (1½ lb) pork shoulder, boneless
2 tablespoons white vinegar
1 tablespoon dark soya sauce
6 shallots or 3 small red onions
1 tablespoon oil
3 cloves garlic, crushed
4 cm (1½ inch) piece fresh ginger, sliced
2 teaspoons grated *lengkuas* (optional)
1 teaspoon dried shrimp paste
8-10 dried chillies, crushed
1 heaped teaspoon mustard seeds, lightly crushed
1 heaped teaspoon fenugreek seeds, lightly crushed
¾ teaspoon turmeric powder, or
   2 teaspoons grated fresh turmeric
1 stalk lemon grass, very finely chopped
6 candlenuts

1¼ cups veal or light beef stock
salt
pepper

Cut pork into 5 cm (2 inch) pieces and sprinkle with a mixture of vinegar and soya sauce. Leave to stand for 30 minutes.

Peel and chop shallots or onions. Heat oil in a large saucepan and fry shallots with crushed garlic for 2 minutes. Add sliced ginger, *lengkuas* (if used), dried shrimp paste, chillies and mustard and fenugreek seeds. Stir on moderate heat for 3 minutes, then add turmeric, lemon grass and ground candlenuts. Put in cubed meat and mix well with the seasonings. Turn heat up to brown meat well.

Pour in stock, season with salt and pepper and cover pan tightly. Cook on a moderate heat until meat is tender. Shake pan occasionally to turn meat, but do not open lid for at least the first 20 minutes of cooking.

If liquid dries up too quickly, sprinkle on a little more stock or water to keep meat moist until cooked. When meat is done, the liquid should be completely absorbed and the pan dry.

MUTTON AND EGGPLANT CURRY

500 g (1 lb) lean mutton or lamb, shoulder or leg
3 medium eggplants
salt
1½ tablespoons white poppy seeds
1 teaspoon fennel seeds, crushed
3 teaspoons coriander, ground
1¼ teaspoons cummin, ground
1½ teaspoons black peppercorns, crushed
¾ teaspoon turmeric powder or
   1½ teaspoons grated fresh turmeric
2.5 cm (1 inch) piece fresh ginger
8 shallots or 3 small red onions
3 cloves garlic
4 tablespoons *ghee* or oil
3 curry leaves, or 1 bay leaf
3 cloves
2 cm (¾ inch) stick cinnamon
2 cups thin coconut milk
½ cup thick coconut milk
lime juice or wedges of fresh lime

Chop meat into 2 cm (¾ inch) cubes. Remove stems from eggplants, wipe with a clean cloth and cut in halves lengthways, then into 5 cm (2 inch) pieces. Sprinkle with salt, cover and allow to stand for 10 minutes to draw bitter juices.

Grind poppy seeds, fennel, coriander, cummin and peppercorns together and mix with turmeric. Peel ginger and shred finely. Mince shallots or onions and garlic. Heat *ghee* or oil in a large pan and fry onions and garlic with ginger for 3 minutes. Add ground seasonings and fry for 5 minutes, stirring frequently. Put in cubed meat, curry or bay leaves, cloves and cinnamon stick. Cook on moderate heat for 10 minutes, stirring to coat meat with seasonings.

Rinse eggplants, wipe and add to the pan, cooking for another 5 minutes. Pour on thin coconut milk and bring almost to the boil. Lower heat and cook for about 25 minutes until meat and eggplant are tender. Stir in

Fruit and Vegetable Salad (recipe page 53), and Vegetables in Coconut Milk (recipe page 52).

thick coconut milk and cook until sauce thickens slightly.

Season to taste with salt and lime juice. Spoon into a serving dish. If serving with lime wedges, arrange around the edge of the dish.

Note: If using mutton, do not add eggplant when frying meat. Simmer meat in thin coconut milk until almost tender, then add eggplant and cook for another 20-25 minutes before adding thick coconut milk.

STEAMBOAT

10 cups chicken stock
½ teaspoon monosodium glutamate (optional)
2 tablespoons vegetable oil
2.5 cm (1 inch) piece fresh ginger, sliced
1 fresh red or green chilli, sliced
8 spring onions, chopped
12 medium raw prawns
125 g (¼ lb) pork, leg or shoulder
125 g (¼ lb) rump, sirloin or fillet steak
125 g (¼ lb) chicken breast
250 g (½ lb) fish fillets (bream, perch, whiting)
125 g (¼ lb) cuttlefish (optional)
large bunch fresh spinach, lettuce or Chinese cabbage leaves
6 eggs (optional)
chilli sauce
3 tablespoons light soya sauce
3 cloves garlic
2.5 cm (1 inch) piece fresh ginger, shredded
2 teaspoons sugar

Bring stock to a rapid boil and add monosodium glutamate (if used), vegetable oil, ginger, sliced chilli and onions. Turn heat down and simmer for 10 minutes, then pour into the Steamboat or other suitable pot which can be heated at the table.

Peel and devein prawns, leaving tails on. Slice pork, beef and chicken thinly. Cut fish fillets into thin strips. Clean and slice cuttlefish. Wash vegetables and shake out excess water. Separate leaves. Arrange meat, prawns and fish attractively on a plate with the vegetables. Keep eggs aside.

Mix soya sauce, crushed garlic, shredded ginger and sugar, stirring till sugar is dissolved. Pour into several small dishes. Spoon chilli sauce into several small dishes.

When stock begins to bubble, the ingredients are cooked individually at the table by each diner, using wooden chopsticks or small wire baskets. Fondue forks could be used. Dip cooked food into either of the sauces.

When all ingredients have been consumed, carefully break the eggs into the stock and poach lightly. These are eaten with the remaining highly enriched soup.

FRIED RICE NOODLES

BEEHOON

375 g (¾ lb) thin rice vermicelli
2 cloves garlic

1½ teaspoons coriander, ground
½ teaspoon turmeric powder
peanut oil
8 dried Chinese mushrooms, soaked
90 g (3 oz) peeled raw prawns
125 g (¼ lb) white fish
2 medium onions
4 fresh red chillies
salt
125 g (¼ lb) beanshoots
2 eggs, lightly beaten
3 spring onions, chopped
fresh coriander sprigs

Soak noodles in cold water for 5 minutes, then drop into boiling water and steep for about 6-10 minutes until soft. Drain well and rinse in cold water.

Crush garlic and make into a paste with coriander and turmeric. Heat 1 tablespoon oil in a *wok* or frying pan and fry seasoning paste for 2 minutes.

Remove mushroom stems and slice mushrooms thinly. Chop prawns and fish into small dice and add to the pan together with mushrooms. Fry on moderate heat for 4 minutes. Remove from pan and keep warm.

Add 2 tablespoons oil to the pan and fry sliced onions and chillies. Add noodles, season with salt and stir thoroughly. Scatter beanshoots on top and cook, covered, for 1 minute. Mix beanshoots into noodles and remove from pan. Pour in beaten egg, swirling pan to make a very thin omelette. Cook until set, then remove and cool slightly. Shred.

Reheat noodles, adding half the seafood and mushrooms and half of the shredded egg to the pan. Lift onto a flat serving dish and garnish with remaining seafood and mushrooms. Top with shredded egg, chopped spring onions and coriander sprigs.

VEGETABLES IN COCONUT MILK

185 g (6 oz) green beans
250 g (½ lb) Chinese cabbage or white cabbage
1½ large onions
2 medium tomatoes
2 fresh red chillies
2 tablespoons vegetable oil
2 cloves garlic, crushed
⅓ teaspoon turmeric powder
½ teaspoon chilli powder (optional)
salt
1¼ cups thin coconut milk
1 tablespoon tamarind water, made with 1½ teaspoons tamarind

Cut beans into 5 cm (2 inch) lengths. Chop Chinese cabbage and wash, shake out excess water. Chop onions roughly, peel and chop tomatoes and slice chillies.

Heat oil in a frying pan and add garlic and chopped onion. Fry for 2 minutes, then put in beans, turmeric, chilli powder (if used), sliced chillies and salt. Pour in ½ cup coconut milk and stir well. Cook on moderate heat for 5 minutes, then add cabbage and cook for a further 4 minutes.

Pour on remaining coconut milk, bring almost to the boil and turn heat down low. Add tomato and tamarind water and simmer for 1-2 minutes. Stir continually to prevent coconut sauce curdling. Add salt to taste.

FRUIT AND VEGETABLE SALAD

RUJAK

¼ yam bean *(bangkuang),* or 1 hard green pear
2 tablespoons oil
1 cake hard beancurd
125 g (¼ lb) beanshoots
1 green mango, or 2 slices green papaya
1 star fruit (carambola), optional
1 small cucumber
6 lettuce leaves
6 thin slices pineapple

Sauce:
1 tablespoon tamarind
½ cup boiling water
2 fresh red chillies, minced
1 tablespoon roasted peanuts, crushed
½ teaspoon dried shrimp paste
1-2 teaspoons sugar
2 tablespoons sweet soya sauce

Prepare sauce first by infusing tamarind in boiling water until softened. Mash pulp, then strain into a small saucepan. Add chilli and peanuts, crumbled dried shrimp paste, sugar and sweet soya sauce. Bring almost to the boil. Check flavour and add more sugar if needed Pour into a sauce boat and set aside.

Shred peeled yam bean (if used), and drop into boiling water. Leave for 10 minutes, then drain. If using pear, peel and shred and sprinkle with a little salt water.

Heat oil and fry beancurd for 2 minutes, lift out and cool. Cut into thin slices. Steep beanshoots in boiling water for 2 minutes, then drain well. Rinse in cold water and drain again. Shred mango or papaya and thinly slice cucumber and star fruit (if used).

Wash lettuce and arrange on a plate. Cut pineapple into small wedges and place around the edge of the dish. Stack all vegetables and fruit in the dish with beancurd on top. Pour on the sauce or serve separately.

CURRY PUFFS

Makes 24.

500 g (1 lb) prepared puff pastry
100 g (3½ oz) beef or mutton
2 medium potatoes
60 g (2 oz) cooked peas
1 medium onion
2 teaspoons finely chopped fresh coriander leaves
1 cm (½ inch) piece fresh ginger, minced
2 cloves garlic, crushed
2 teaspoons coriander seeds
¼ teaspoon fennel (optional)
1½ teaspoon cummin seeds
2 dried chillies
1 cm (½ inch) stick cinnamon
1 clove
1 teaspoon black peppercorns
1 teaspoon turmeric powder
2 tablespoons *ghee*
1 small onion
2 teaspoons salt
oil for deep frying (optional)

If pastry is frozen, allow to thaw. Chop or mince beef or mutton. Peel potatoes, boil until tender, cool and dice. Drain peas. Chop onion finely. Pound all spices and seasonings into a paste.

Heat *ghee* and fry onion for 3 minutes, add seasoning paste and fry for 4 minutes. Stir in minced meat and cook until well coloured. Stir in potato and peas, heat through, then add chopped tomato and salt. Cover and cook for 4-5 minutes on low heat, stirring frequently to prevent sticking. Remove from heat, and cool completely.

Roll out pastry to 2 mm (1/16 inch) thickness. Divide into 24 circles 10 cm (4 inches) in diameter using a pastry cutter. Place a small amount of filling on one side of each pastry circle. Fold over to form semi-circular pastries. Stick edges down with a little milk or water. Run a pastry wheel around the join, or pinch the wedges into a fluted pattern all around.

Heat oil and deep fry Curry Puffs to a golden brown. Remove from oil, drain and serve either hot or cold. Alternatively, heat oven to 200°C/400°F/Gas Mark 6. Brush pastry tops with a little beaten egg or milk, avoiding sealed edges. Place on a baking sheet and bake for 20-25 minutes. Cool slightly, then remove to a wire rack. Serve hot or cold.

GULA MELAKA PUDDING

125 g (¼ lb) pearl sago
4½ cups water
155 g (5 oz) crumbled palm sugar *(gula Melaka),* or
     185 g (6 oz) brown sugar
¾ cup hot water
1 *pandan* leaf (optional)
1¼ cups thick coconut milk

Wash sago, drain, and put into a saucepan. Add water and bring to the boil. Turn heat down and cook until sago is tender and each grain clear. Rinse with several lots of cold water to separate grains, then divide between small glass bowls or jelly moulds and place in the refrigerator to chill.

Put palm sugar into a small pan, add crushed *pandan* leaf (if used), and pour on hot water. Simmer for 6 minutes. Strain and discard leaf.

If brown sugar is used, place in a small saucepan with ⅔ cup water and bring to the boil. Stir to dissolve sugar and cook on high heat until syrup is quite sticky and has begun to caramelise to a deep brown. Remove from heat. Carefully pour in ¼ cup cold water, holding saucepan well away to avoid burns from the spluttering syrup. Cover hands with a cloth before doing this. Stir well and allow to cool, then chill.

To serve dessert, pour a little sugar syrup and coconut milk over each dish of sago. Add a little shaved ice if desired. Garnish with a mint leaf.

JAPAN

BASIC STOCK

DASHI

1 piece dried kelp *(kombu),* about 5 cm (2 inches)
    square
4 cups water
15 g (½ oz) dried bonito flakes *(katsuobushi)*

Simmer *kombu* and water together for 3 minutes. Remove *kombu* and sprinkle dried bonito flakes over the water. Let stand undisturbed for 2 minutes, then strain. Will keep in the refrigerator for 2-3 days.

MISO SOUP

MISO SHIRU

1 piece dried kelp *(kombu)* 2.5 cm (1 inch) square
    (optional)
2¾ cups *dashi* stock
100 g (3½ oz) diced chicken or fish
75 g (2½ oz) diced beancurd
4 tablespoons white *miso* paste
2 teaspoons sugar
pinch of monosodium glutamate (optional)
4 spring onions, finely chopped
6 sprigs watercress

Put *kombu* in a large pot with stock and bring to the boil. Add chicken and boil for 5 minutes. Remove *kombu* and discard, then add diced beancurd. If fish is used instead of chicken, add at this time. Simmer for 2 minutes.

Scoop out ½ cup of the hot stock and blend with *miso* and sugar. Stir this into the soup with monosodium glutamate (if used). Simmer for 4 minutes. Serve in covered lacquered soup bowls, garnished with shredded spring onions and a sprig of watercress.

SALMON SAUTEED WITH LEMON

LEMON YAKI

750 g (1½ lb) salmon or salmon trout
1 teaspoon salt
oil or butter
2 lemons
2 small cucumbers, about 13 cm (5 inches) long

Cut salmon into six streaks, across the body. Sprinkle with salt and let stand for several minutes. Rinse off and wipe dry. In a heavy-based pan heat oil or butter and saute fish gently for 4 minutes on each side. Sprinkle with juice of 1 lemon during cooking. When fish is cooked, lift each slice onto a small plate, preferably rectangular, and decorate with cucumber fans and lemon butterflies prepared as follows.

Wash cucumbers and cut each into 3 pieces. Slice each piece lengthways into 0.5 cm (¼ inch) slices, discarding end pieces. To make cucumber fans, use a very sharp knife to cut each slice into strips, leaving the end 0.5 cm (¼ inch) uncut. Gently press the 'fan' ribs open.

Slice remaining lemon into thin slices and make butterfly shapes by cutting away a small triangle from two opposite sides, leaving wing-like shapes.

ASSORTED RAW FISH PLATE

SASHIMI NORIAWASI

90 g (3 oz) tuna fillet
90 g (3 oz) bream
60 g (2 oz) salmon
60 g (2 oz) freshwater trout
3 medium cuttlefish (squid)
2 pieces dried laver *(nori),* each 15 cm by 10 cm
    (6 inches by 4 inches)
6 medium raw prawns
6 raw scallops or clams (optional)
1 small cucumber
¼ giant white radish
white vinegar
salt
sugar
lemon peel
8 cm (3 inch) piece fresh ginger
small lettuce leaves
watercress sprigs
powdered green horseradish *(wasabi),* or freshly grated
    horseradish
lemon juice
light soya sauce

For good Sashimi it is essential that all fish and shellfish are absolutely fresh, preferably bought live from the market where possible. Though the dish calls for raw fish, in the interest of hygiene, any surface bacteria can be eliminated by dipping the sliced portions of fish or shellfish into a bowl of very hot water and then into a dish of iced water. Drain well and wipe with a kitchen towel before using.

Remove skin from tuna and cut diagonally to the grain into 1 cm (½ inch) thick slices, then into pieces about 4 cm by 2.5 cm (1½ inches by 1 inch). Slice salmon and bream thinly and cut into 2.5 cm (1 inch) squares. Skin may be left on bream. Remove any bones from trout, skin, then cut into narrow strips and tie into simple knots.

Wash cuttlefish, peel off skin and cut away head and ink bag. Clean out and rinse well. Using a sharp knife, cut one cuttlefish into thin circles, discarding tentacles if these are not considered appetising. Cut the other two open and press flat. Score with a criss-cross pattern on one side.

Hold dried laver over a flame to crisp slightly, then

Egg Custard in Teacups (recipe page 60), Quail Eggs, Chicken Meatballs and Pickled Cucumbers on Skewers (recipe page 58), and Green Beans with Sesame Dressing (recipe page 61).

press onto the cuttlefish on the unscored sides. Roll up tightly and cut into 2.5 cm (1 inch) pieces. When serving, stand these on end to expose the alternate colours of white and green.

Shell prawns, leaving tail fins intact. Remove dark veins and slit open underneath the prawns. Press flat. Parboil or sprinkle with a little lemon or ginger juice. Rinse scallops or clams in salted water and cut into thin slices.

Wash cucumber and rub with salt. Shred finely and marinate in a sweet mixture of 1 tablespoon vinegar, 3 teaspoons sugar and ½ teaspoon salt for 5 minutes. Drain.

Peel white radish, cut into 2.5 cm (1 inch) blocks. With a small sharp knife shred the top section to form 'chrysanthemum flower' decorations. Place a sliver of lemon peel in the centre of each 'flower'.

Peel and shred ginger. Wash lettuce and watercress and shake out water.

On a large platter or several smaller ones, arrange the fish and shellfish attractively. Decorate with shredded cucumber and ginger, the radish flowers and sprigs of watercress. Place lettuce leaves beneath prawns, scallops and clams.

Prepare sauces by mixing the following:

Sauce 1:
¼ cup light soya sauce
2 tablespoons lemon juice

Sauce 2:
⅓ cup light soya sauce
1 tablespoon powdered green horseradish, or freshly grated horseradish

Serve the sauces in small bowls. Dip fish into one of the sauces before eating.

FISH AND BAMBOO SHOOTS

NITSUKE

1 medium carrot, thinly sliced
salt
6 thick slices white fish (cod, snapper, haddock)
1 cup *dashi* or fish stock
⅔ cup *mirin*
1 tablespoon sugar
2 tablespoons light soya sauce
155 g (5 oz) canned bamboo shoots, thinly sliced

Place carrot in a small saucepan and cover with slightly salted water. Bring to the boil, turn heat down and simmer until cooked but still crisp. Drain and cool. Set aside.

Arrange fish in a wide pan, pour on stock and *mirin* and simmer on low heat for 3 minutes, then sprinkle on sugar and soya sauce, shaking pan to dissolve the sugar and mix the sauce. Cook until fish is tender, then lift onto a heated plate. Add bamboo shoots to the pan and simmer in sauce for 2-3 minutes.

Place one piece of fish and several pieces of bamboo shoot in small bowls. Dip carrot pieces in the remaining sauce, then add to the bowls. Pour about 1 tablespoon sauce over each fish slice.

SEAFOOD HOTPOT

YOSENABE

3 small potatoes, or 2 small sweet potatoes
24 gingko nuts (optional)
500 g (1 lb) white fish fillets
90 g (3 oz) raw shrimp or prawns
90 g (3 oz) raw clams or scallops
250 g (½ lb) *kamaboko* (fish cake) or mild flavoured sausage
½ head Chinese cabbage
250 g (½ lb) spinach or mustard greens
8-10 dried Japanese black mushrooms, soaked in cold water for ½ hour
1 carrot, thinly sliced
100 g (3½ oz) *shirataki* noodles
6 cups *dashi* stock
light soya sauce
salt

Peel potatoes or sweet potatoes and cut into 1 cm (½ inch) thick slices. Parch gingko nuts, if used, in a hot oven or under the grill, then rub off skins, holding the hot nuts in a kitchen towel.

Slice fish into pieces about 5 cm (2 inches) square. Peel and devein shrimp or prawns. Wash clams or scallops in slightly salted water and cut in halves.

Slice *kamaboko* or sausage thinly. Rinse vegetables and chop coarsely. Drain soaked mushrooms and cut a cross in the cap of each.

Pour *dashi* stock into a large earthenware or fireproof pot and bring to the boil. (A very light chicken stock can be used in place of *dashi*, but the essential seaweed and fish flavour would be missing, making this a rather tasteless dish by comparison.) When stock begins to bubble, add potato and cook on high heat for 8-10 minutes, or until the vegetable begins to soften. Sweet potato will require less cooking time.

Add the green vegetables, carrot, gingko nuts and mushrooms. Turn heat down slightly and cook for 5 minutes, then add noodles, fish, shrimp, clams or scallops and *kamaboko* or sausage. Cover the pot and turn heat down very low. Simmer for about 4 minutes, then take the pot to the table and set it over a portable fire or fondue spirit fire.

Season to taste with soya sauce and salt. If available, Japanese *sansho*, a blend of powdered Japanese peppers, should be sprinkled over the dish.

GRILLED EEL

UNAGI KABAYAKI

750 g (1½ lb) fresh eel
2 tablespoons oil
¼ cup *mirin*
¼ cup light soya sauce
shredded cucumber or giant white radish

With a sharp knife cut skin around the head of the eel and pull off the skin in one piece. Slice eel open, cut away backbone and cut meat into 8 cm (3 inch) pieces. Flatten and brush with oil.

Place under the grill and cook on moderate heat, for

at least 5 minutes on each side, brushing occasionally with oil. Combine *mirin* and soya sauce in a small saucepan and bring to the boil. Dip eel pieces in the sauce and return to the grill to cook until the glaze begins to dry. Brush with more glaze and continue cooking, adding more glaze until the eel is done and the sauce used up.

Place eel pieces on a serving dish and garnish with shredded cucumber or radish.

DEEP FRIED SEAFOOD AND VEGETABLES

TEMPURA

1 small sweet potato or 1 slice pumpkin
1 medium carrot
6 green beans
2 small green peppers
1 small eggplant
salt
12 spring onions
6 chrysanthemum leaves (optional)
125 g (¼ lb) thin white fish fillets
125 g (¼ lb) cuttlefish
12 medium raw prawns, in shells
1½ teaspoons ginger juice
½ teaspoon sugar
pinch of salt
cornflour
vegetable oil
1 teaspoon sesame oil

Batter:
500 g (1 lb) plain flour
3 tablespoons cornflour
3 eggs
cold water

Sauce:
1 cup *dashi* stock
½ cup light soya sauce
½ cup *mirin*
2 tablespoons grated giant white radish
sesame seeds (optional)

Peel sweet potato or pumpkin and cut into 0.5 cm (¼ inch) slices. Rub with a little salt. Peel and slice carrot. Cut beans into 5 cm (2 inch) lengths. Wipe peppers and cut into 2.5 cm (1 inch) squares. Wipe eggplant and cut into 0.5 cm (¼ inch) slices and sprinkle with salt. Cut 10 cm (4 inch) pieces from white part of spring onions. Wash and wipe chrysanthemum leaves (if used).

Cut fish into 5 cm (2 inch) squares. Skin cuttlefish and cut into thin circles or flatten and score a criss-cross pattern across one surface. Remove heads and shells from prawns leaving tail fins on. Clip fins. Sprinkle fish, cuttle fish and prawns with a mixture of ginger juice, sugar and salt.

Make a medium to thin batter with flour, cornflour, eggs and cold water. Beat for 1 minute, but leave very slightly lumpy. Set aside for 10 minutes.

Pour *dashi,* soya sauce and *mirin* into a saucepan and heat gently, then remove and leave to cool. When cold,

add grated radish and a sprinkling of sesame seeds and pour into small dipping dishes.

Heat oil for deep frying. Add sesame oil. Dip vegetable pieces into the batter and place several at a time in the hot oil. Fry until well coloured and cooked through. Drain on absorbent paper. Coat fish, prawns and cuttlefish with cornflour, shake off excess and coat with the batter. Fry until golden and cooked through.

Arrange the seafood and vegetables attractively on a serving dish and serve at once. Ideally, Tempura should be eaten piece by piece as it is cooked. If possible fry in a portable pan on or near the table. Dip the Tempura in sauce before eating.

PRAWNS BAKED IN SEA SALT

24 very large raw prawns
2 tablespoons *sake*
625 g (1¼ lb) sea salt
bamboo or metal skewers

Sauce:
For each serving mix the following:
½ teaspoon powdered green horseradish *(wasabi)*
2 teaspoons *dashi* stock
2 tablespoons light soya sauce

Peel prawns, leaving heads and tail fins intact. Devein. Arrange on a flat platter and sprinkle with *sake*. Stand for 2 hours.

Wipe prawns with paper towels and insert skewers along the bodies from tail to head. Coat each thickly with salt, pressing on firmly. Put on a baking tray which is covered with a thin layer of salt. Sprinkle a little more salt on top and bake for about 12 minutes in a fairly hot oven (220°C/425°F/Gas Mark 7). Alternatively cook over a charcoal barbecue for about 10 minutes.

Wipe off salt and arrange prawns on a serving dish. Put sauce in individual sauce dishes and serve with the prawns.

GRILLED CHICKEN

YAKITORI

6 chicken thighs
⅓ cup *sake*
⅓ cup dark soya sauce
60 g (2 oz) sugar
¼ cup *mirin*
2 teaspoons powdered ginger
¼ giant white radish or 1 small cucumber
salt
6 bamboo or metal skewers

Wash chicken thighs, wipe dry and insert skewers securely along bones. Cook over a charcoal barbecue or under a moderate grill until partially done.

Mix *sake,* soya sauce, sugar and *mirin* and pour into a wide, flat bowl. Lay the chicken thighs in the sauce for 5 minutes, turn and marinate other side for 5 minutes. Return to the griller or barbecue and cook for 2 minutes on each side.

Return to the sauce, then grill again, this time brushing the chicken with the remaining sauce while chicken cooks and sauce forms a dark, shiny glaze. Sprinkle on powdered ginger.

Shred radish or cucumber and sprinkle with salt. Arrange chicken thighs on small plates and garnish each with a small mound of radish or cucumber.

BEEF HOTPOT

SHABU SHABU

1 kg (2 lb) steak (sirloin, rump or striploin)
500 g (1 lb) spinach, watercress, cabbage or lettuce
12 fresh mushrooms
250 g (½ lb) canned bamboo shoots, drained
2 medium carrots
12 spring onions
3 squares soft beancurd, quartered
6 cups *dashi* or soup stock
1 large piece dried kelp *(kombu)* (optional)
500 g (1 lb) thick egg noodles or spaghetti, partially cooked
3 tablespoons spring onion or Japanese leek, finely chopped
chilli powder, or *sansho* to taste

Sauce 1:
3 teaspoons light soya sauce
1 teaspoon powdered green horseradish *(wasabi)*

Mix well and serve in individual bowls.

Sauce 2:
45 g (1½ oz) white sesame seeds
1 cup *dashi* stock
¾ cup light soya sauce
2 teaspoons sesame oil
2 tablespoons lemon juice
2 teaspoons finely chopped red chilli

Toast sesame seeds under a griller, then grind and mix with all other ingredients in a small saucepan. Bring to the boil, remove from heat and cool. Pour into small bowls.

To prepare Shabu Shabu, slice beef across the grain into wafer-thin slices. Clean green vegetables and cut leaves in halves. If using watercress break into sprigs. Remove mushroom stems and peel or wipe caps. Slice bamboo shoots thinly and cut carrots into thin discs. Remove roots and green tops from spring onions and cut into 5 cm (2 inch) pieces.

Divide meat between six wooden platters and place vegetables and beancurd on one or two serving dishes in the centre of the table near the hotpot. Pour stock into the pot, add kelp and bring to the boil. If the fire is not strong enough, bring stock to the boil before bringing to the table. Using wooden chopsticks or fondue forks, hold meat in bubbling stock until cooked to individual taste, ideally very rare. Dip in either of the sauces before eating.

When most of the beef is cooked, add some vegetables and beancurd and cook briefly. When all meat and vegetables are finished, remove kelp and add noodles to the broth. Cook until soft, then spoon into soup bowls. Sprinkle on chopped spring onion or leek

and chilli powder or *sansho* and add ladle of the enriched soup.

BRAISED PORK AND LEEK ROLLS

TERIYAKI

6 leeks or 12 Japanese leeks
6 very thin slices pork shoulder or leg
⅓ cup light soya sauce
⅓ cup *sake* or *mirin*
2 tablespoons sugar
vegetable oil
2 small cucumbers
2 tablespoons white vinegar
2 teaspoons salt
3 teaspoons sugar

Wash leeks, remove roots and green tops and cut pieces the same length as the width of each slice of pork. Wrap pork securely around one piece of leek or two pieces of Japanese leek and secure with toothpicks.

Mix soya sauce, *sake* or *mirin* and sugar, stirring until sugar dissolves. Heat 2.5 cm (1 inch) oil in a frying pan and cook rolls on moderate heat, turning to brown evenly.

Wash and dry cucumbers, cut into wedges about 2.5 cm (1 inch) long and sprinkle with a mixture of vinegar, salt and sugar. Set aside to marinate for a few minutes.

Drain oil from pan when pork is partially cooked and pour in prepared sauce. Simmer on low heat for 6-7 minutes, turning pork frequently. Remove Teriyaki from the pan and cut each piece into two or three pieces. Stand these upright on small, flat plates and garnish each with several pieces of drained cucumber.

Bring remaining sauce to the boil and cook until reduced to a thick glaze. Spoon a little over each portion of Teriyaki before serving.

QUAIL EGGS, CHICKEN MEATBALLS AND PICKLED CUCUMBER ON SKEWERS

Chicken meatballs:
250 g (½ lb) minced, cooked chicken
2 egg whites
½ teaspoon salt
pinch of pepper
vegetable oil
1 teaspoon sugar
3 teaspoons dark soya sauce
2 teaspoons *mirin*
1 tablespoon orange juice

For skewers:
1 medium cucumber
2 tablespoons vinegar
1 teaspoon salt
12 quail eggs (or 6 small hen eggs)
12 thin bamboo skewers
shredded lettuce or cabbage (optional)

To prepare chicken meatballs, blend the minced chicken and egg whites thoroughly. Season with salt and

Braised Pork and Leek Rolls (recipe this page).

pepper. Using wet hands form the paste into 24 small balls. Heat about 2.5 cm (1 inch) oil in a frying pan and fry meatballs to a deep golden colour. Remove from the pan and drain on absorbent paper.

Remove oil from the pan and pour in sugar, soya sauce, *mirin* and orange juice. Stir on low heat till sugar dissolves, then return the meatballs to the pan and turn slowly in the sauce. Simmer gently, shaking the pan to turn meatballs constantly, until sauce forms a glaze on the meatballs. Turn off heat and allow meatballs to cool.

To prepare skewers, wipe cucumber and cut into 12 pieces. Put in a flat dish and sprinkle on vinegar and salt. Stand for 10 minutes, turning once. Put quail eggs in a saucepan, cover with cold water and bring to the boil. Turn heat down a little and boil eggs for 6 minutes. If using small hen eggs boil for 8 minutes. Drain off hot water, then cover with cold water. When eggs are cold, drain and shell. Cut small eggs in halves (if used).

Thread onto each skewer one meatball, a piece of cucumber, a quail egg (or half a small egg) and another meatball. Arrange on a bed of finely shredded lettuce or cabbage, or place on attractively folded paper napkins. Serve as part of the main meal, or as *hors d'oeuvres*.

OMELETTE ROLL

DASHIMAKI TAMAGO

6 eggs
3 tablespoons sugar
1 teaspoon salt
1½ tablespoons *mirin*
½ cup *dashi* stock
pinch of monosodium glutamate (optional)
1 teaspoon light soya sauce
vegetable oil
6 sprigs watercress or parsley
½ small cucumber
salt
white vinegar

Beat 3 eggs lightly and add half the sugar, salt, *mirin*, *dashi*, monosodium glutamate (if used) and soya sauce. Beat for 2 minutes. Heat a little oil in an omelette pan and pour in one-third of the mixture. Cook on moderate to low heat and when omelette is just set, carefully lift onto a plate or a piece of greaseproof paper. Cook remaining batter in two parts and stack the three omelettes together. Roll up carefully and return to the pan to cook on low heat for a further 2 minutes. Lift from pan and wrap in a piece of clean muslin, tying securely to form a firm roll. Cool.

Repeat the process with the remaining eggs and seasonings, and wrap in another piece of muslin. When both rolls are completely cool, remove cloth and cut each roll into three pieces.

Wash watercress or parsely. Rub cucumber with a little salt, then steep in boiling water for 2 minutes. Drain, cool and cut into 5 cm (2 inch) pieces. Sprinkle with a little salt and vinegar. Stand pieces of omelette roll on end on a serving dish, garnish each with a sprig of watercress or parsley and decorate the plate with cucumber.

Serve as a breakfast dish or as the first course of a main meal.

EGG CUSTARD IN TEACUPS

CHAWAN MUSHI

6 eggs
6 dried Japanese black mushrooms, soaked in cold water for ½ hour
90 g (3 oz) chicken
1 tablespoon light soya sauce
½ small cucumber
salt
1¾ cups *dashi* stock
2 teaspoons *mirin*
pinch of monosodium glutamate (optional)
30 g (1 oz) fish or raw clams, diced
6 small peeled raw shrimp
6 sprigs parsley or watercress leaves

Beat eggs lightly in a mixing bowl. Remove stems from mushrooms. Dice chicken and marinate in soya sauce for 10 minutes. Rub cucumber with a little salt, then slice lengthways into 6 pieces, remove seeds.

Add *dashi*, 1 teaspoon salt, *mirin* and monosodium glutamate to eggs and beat again. Put chicken, fish and 1 mushroom into 6 Japanese teacups or small ramekins and pour in egg mixture. Set in a steamer and cook over high heat until almost set.

Press a shrimp and a parsley sprig or watercress leaf onto the top of each custard and cook for a further 10 minutes. Serve with sliced cucumber.

NOODLES WITH CHICKEN AND VEGETABLES

NABEYAKI UDON

750 g (1½ lb) *udon* noodles, or spaghetti
6 cups *dashi* or chicken stock
6 dried Japanese black mushrooms, soaked in cold water for ½ hour
12 spring onions
90 g (3 oz) chicken breast
½ teaspoon monosodium glutamate (optional)
⅔ cup light soya sauce
⅔ cup *mirin* or *sake*
1½ teaspoons sugar
60 g (2 oz) fish cake *(kamaboko)*, sliced (optional)
6 eggs
sansho or chilli powder

Soak noodles for 20 minutes in cold water. Drain. Bring stock to the oil. Add noodles and cook till tender. Remove noodles from the stock, drain and spread on a tray to dry slightly.

Drain mushrooms and remove stems. Clean spring onions and cut into 2.5 cm (1 inch) pieces. Remove any skin and bones from chicken and slice thinly. Return stock to moderate heat. Add chicken and mushrooms and cook until chicken is tender. Remove chicken and mushrooms from soup with a perforated spoon and set aside. Season soup with monosodium glutamate (if used), soya sauce, *mirin* and sugar. Add spring onions and *kamaboko*, if used.

Return noodles, reheat, then divide noodles and soup between six large bowls. Add a mushroom and several pieces of chicken to each bowl. Break an egg on top of the noodles and add a sprinkling of *sansho* or chilli powder. Cover bowls and put in a hot oven, or on warming plate for 5 minutes before serving.

VINEGARED RICE

CHIRASHI ZUSHI

375 g (¾ lb) short grain white rice
3 cups water
1 small cucumber
salt
white vinegar
sugar
90 g (3 oz) white fish fillet
2 eggs, beaten
vegetable oil
90 g (3 oz) cooked peas
1 tablespoon shredded preserved ginger

Seasoning Sauce:
4 tablespoons white vinegar
2 tablespoons sugar
1½ teaspoons salt

Wash rice, put into a heavy-based saucepan, cover with water and cook, covered, on low heat till tender. Set aside.

Wipe cucumber and rub with a little salt. Shred or grate, then marinate in a mixture of 3 teaspoons vinegar and 1 teaspoon sugar.

Steam or boil fish fillet till soft, then flake or chop coarsely. Sprinkle on a mixture of 3 teaspoons vinegar, 1½ teaspoons sugar and ½ teaspoon salt.

Mix eggs with 2 teaspoons sugar and ½ teaspoon salt and pour into a hot, lightly oiled pan. Cook until firm, turn and cook other side, then remove and cool. When cool, shred with a sharp knife.

Mix seasoning sauce, stirring until sugar is completely dissolved. Pour into rice and mix in with a chopstick, then fold in fish, cucumber, shredded egg and peas. Garnish with shredded ginger.

GREEN BEANS WITH SESAME DRESSING

INGEN NO GOMA-AE

250 g (½ lb) young green beans
3 tablespoons white sesame seeds
1 tablespoon sesame oil
½ teaspoon sugar
1 teaspoon *mirin*

Cook beans, left whole, in boiling, slightly salted water until tender, but not too soft. Drain and cool. Cut into

5 cm (2 inch) pieces and place in small dishes or a salad bowl.

Toast sesame seeds lightly, then grind to a paste with sesame oil, sugar and *mirin*. Spoon over the beans, stirring lightly with a chopstick to mix. Serve cold.

CUCUMBER SALAD

KYURIMOMI

3 small cucumbers
2 teaspoons salt
2 tablespoons white vinegar
1 tablespoon water
1 teaspoon light soya sauce
½ teaspoon salt
2 teaspoons sugar
½ teaspoon dried chilli flakes
1 teaspoon sesame oil
pinch of monosodium glutamate (optional)

Wash cucumbers and rub with salt. Slice or cut into thin strips as preferred. Mix remaining ingredients together, stirring to dissolve sugar. Put cucumber in a salad bowl and pour on dressing. Toss well, then let stand for 30 minutes in the refrigerator before serving.

PANCAKES FILLED WITH RED BEAN JAM

DORAYAKI

Makes 18.

155 g (5 oz) plain flour
⅔ cup milk
¼ cup water
2 tablespoons butter or oil
2 eggs
1 teaspoon salt
3 teaspoons sugar
1 quantity *yokan* (red bean jam)

Yokan (red bean jam):
220 g (7 oz) mashed cooked red beans
7/8 cup water
125 g (¼ lb) sugar
½ teaspoon salt
3 tablespoons cornflour

Make *yokan* first. Mix mashed beans with water, sugar and salt in a saucepan, stir in cornflour mixed with a little water and cook on low heat for about 10-12 minutes until it becomes a thick paste. Allow to cool while pancakes are prepared.

Blend all pancake ingredients together, beating well. Set aside for 10 minutes. Heat a heavy-based iron skillet or omelette pan and wipe with an oiled cloth. Pour in enough batter to make 8 cm (3 inch) pancakes and cook lightly on both sides. Cook all the batter in this way.

When all pancakes are cooked, spread half with the *yokan* and sandwich with the remaining pancakes. Serve warm or cold. A little sugar may be sprinkled over pancakes before serving.

CHINA

CHICKEN AND SWEET CORN SOUP

375 g (¾ lb) chicken breast
375 g (¾ lb) canned cream-style sweet corn
2 teaspoons salt
1 tablespoon light soya sauce
¼ teaspoon white pepper
2 egg whites
3 spring onions
1 clove garlic (optional)
4 cups chicken stock
cornflour
chopped fresh coriander leaves

Remove skin from chicken breast and cut into very small dice. Pour sweet corn into a saucepan and season with salt, soya sauce and white pepper. Gently heat through. Lightly beat egg whites. Chop onions and garlic very finely.

Bring chicken stock to boil in a large saucepan and add onion, garlic and chicken pieces. Boil for 3 minutes, then pour in beaten egg white. Stir gently so egg forms white strings in the soup. Add warmed cream-style sweet corn and stir thoroughly. Thicken soup if necessary with cornflour mixed with a little cold water. Check seasonings. Garnish with chopped fresh coriander and serve with extra soya sauce.

SOUR AND HOT SZECHWAN SOUP

125 g (¼ lb) frying steak
60 g (2 oz) chicken
2 teaspoons light soya sauce
2 teaspoons Chinese rice wine
3 eggs
3 cloves garlic
1 cm (½ inch) piece fresh ginger
7 cups beef stock or water
pinch of monosodium glutamate (optional)
2 tablespoons dark soya sauce
1 teaspoon salt
1 teaspoon chilli oil
1 teaspoon ground black pepper, or crushed Chinese
    brown peppercorns
1 tablespoon cornflour
6 dried Chinese mushrooms, soaked
2 squares soft beancurd
Chinese brown vinegar

Slice beef and chicken paper thin, then cut into shreds and sprinkle with light soya sauce and Chinese wine. Leave to stand for 10 minutes. Beat eggs lightly and set aside. Mince garlic and ginger and sprinkle over the beef and chicken.

Bring stock or water to the boil, add monosodium glutamate (if used), dark soya sauce, salt, pepper, chilli oil and cornflour mixed with a little of the cold stock or water. Cook for 3 minutes over high heat, then add beef and chicken and cook until the meat is very tender.

Slowly pour in beaten egg to form threads in the soup. Flavour to taste with vinegar, then add thinly sliced mushrooms and diced beancurd. Cook for 2 minutes. Transfer to a serving bowl. Serve with additional Chinese brown vinegar.

FISH SOUP WITH CELERY

375 g (¾ lb) white fish fillets
4 sticks celery
1 teaspoon salt
pinch of white pepper
1 teaspoon Chinese rice wine
½ teaspoon sugar
1 tablespoon light soya sauce
2 tablespoons cornflour
1 tablespoon dried shrimps, soaked for 3 hours
2 cm (¾ inch) piece fresh ginger, sliced
5 cups boiling water
1 fish head (optional)

Cut fillets into thin slices. Quarter celery. Mix salt, pepper, wine, sugar and soya sauce together and rub into sliced fish. Leave for 10 minutes. Put cornflour into a plastic bag and drop in fish slices. Shake bag to coat fish thickly with cornflour.

Put dried shrimps and ginger into a large saucepan with celery, boiling water and the fish head (if used). Bring to boil and simmer for 2 minutes. Drop in fish slices and simmer for 4 minutes. Discard head before serving, if preferred. Check seasoning and serve hot.

WINTER MELON POND

4 kg (8 lb) winter melon
salt
375 g (¾ lb) chicken
100 g (3½ oz) chicken livers
100 g (3½ oz) chicken giblets
60 g (2 oz) fresh crab meat
60 g (2 oz) frozen peas
12 dried Chinese mushrooms, soaked
30 g (1 oz) dried lotus seeds (optional)
50 g (1¾ oz) raw smoked Yunan ham
2 tablespoons cornflour
2 tablespoons oil
salt
light soya sauce

Remove the top of the melon and cut edge in a zig-zag or scalloped design. Carve decorative figures and patterns on the sides. Scoop out seeds and fill the melon with salted water. Stand upright in a steamer and steam over gentle heat for ½ hour.

Remove any skin and bones from chicken and cut into small dice. Clean and slice livers and giblets. Cut crab meat into pieces. Thaw peas. Drain and soak mushrooms. Boil lotus seeds until tender. Shred ham finely and set aside as garnish. Coat chicken pieces lightly in cornflour and fry in oil until lightly coloured. Put into the melon pond and continue to steam.

Scoop a little water from the melon and put into a small saucepan with chicken livers and gizzards, crab meat, peas, mushrooms and lotus seeds. Boil until all are tender, then add to the melon pond. Season to taste with salt and light soya sauce. Stand the melon upright in a large bowl or rack which will hold it securely in place. Scatter on shredded ham before serving.

STEAMED WHOLE FISH WITH GINGER AND GREEN ONION

1 whole bream or perch weighing 500 g (1 lb)
1½ teaspoons Chinese rice wine
½ teaspoon salt
¼ teaspoon white pepper
6 spring onions
4 cm (1½ inch) piece fresh ginger, shredded
1½ teaspoons oil
2 teaspoons light soya sauce
sprigs of fresh coriander

Clean fish, removing scales and intestines. Rinse well, wipe dry, then make several deep diagonal cuts across each side. Sprinkle on Chinese wine and stand for 10 minutes. Rub fish with salt and pepper and put on a lightly oiled plate. Shred spring onions and place half inside the fish together with half of the ginger. Scatter remaining onion and ginger onto the fish. Sprinkle on oil and soya sauce and a very little water.

Cover and cook over high heat in a steamer for about 10 minutes until fish is tender. Test if the fish is done by piercing the thickest part with a thin skewer. If the flesh appears slightly flaky and no pink liquid runs out the fish is done. Do not overcook. Lift onto a serving plate, pour on the cooking liquid and garnish with fresh coriander.

SPICY FISH SLICES

375 g (¾ lb) fish fillets
1 tablespoon dark soya sauce
2 tablespoons light soya sauce
1 tablespoon Chinese rice wine
1 cm (½ inch) piece fresh ginger, shredded
2 cloves garlic
6 spring onions, shredded
75 g (2½ oz) sugar
2 teaspoons salt
1 teaspoon Chinese five-spice powder
¾ cup boiling water
oil
6-8 lettuce leaves

Slice fish into 5 cm (2 inch) squares. Prepare a marinade by mixing soya sauce, wine, ginger, garlic and spring onions. Arrange fish pieces in a shallow flat bowl and pour on the marinade. Let stand for 3 hours, turning occasionally.

Mix sugar, salt, five-spice powder and boiling water in a small saucepan and bring to the boil. Turn heat down very low and keep warm.

Heat 2.5 cm (1 inch) oil in a frying pan or *wok* and fry fish slices over high heat until a dark golden colour on both sides. Lift out from pan on a slotted spoon and return to the marinade dish. Pour on the warm spiced liquid and marinate in this for 5 minutes.

Dip lettuce into a pot of boiling water to which 1 tablespoon oil has been added. Arrange on a warmed serving plate. Drain fish and place on the lettuce. Serve immediately.

SWEET AND SOUR FISH FINGERS

375 g (¾ lb) thick fish fillets
½ teaspoon salt
pinch white pepper
1 teaspoon ginger wine (see glossary)
2 teaspoons cornflour
1 teaspoon sesame oil
125 g (¼ lb) plain flour
60 g (2 oz) cornflour
2 teaspoons baking powder
2 teaspoons oil
oil for deep frying

Sauce:
½ cup white vinegar
75 g (2½ oz) brown sugar
1 tablespoon tomato paste
1 tablespoon dark soya sauce
¾ cup light chicken stock
2 teaspoons cornflour
4 drops red food colouring
pinch of salt
1 cm (½ inch) piece fresh ginger, shredded
2 cloves garlic (optional)
2 spring onions
½ small carrot
15 g (½ oz) canned bamboo shoot
1 small fresh red chilli
30 g (1 oz) celery

Cut fish into pieces about 10 cm by 2.5 cm (4 inches by 1 inch) and dry with kitchen paper. Sprinkle with salt, pepper, ginger wine, cornflour and sesame oil and leave to marinate for 10 minutes.

Prepare sauce by mixing ingredients from vinegar to salt in a small saucepan. Add shredded ginger. Chop garlic and spring onions finely and add to the pan. Scrape and shred carrot, drain and shred bamboo shoot, slice chilli and shred celery. Add all vegetables to the pan. Bring to the boil, stirring until the mixture clears and thickens. Boil for 4 minutes. Keep hot until needed.

Make a batter with plain flour, cornflour, baking powder, oil and enough water to make a batter of dropping consistency. Heat oil until smoking hot. Lower heat to medium. Dip fish into the batter and fry until cooked. Drain and place on a serving dish.

Serve the sauce separately, or pour over the fish pieces just before serving.

FISH WITH HOT BEAN SAUCE

1 whole bream, snapper, or golden carp, weighing
   500 g (1 lb)
oil
1 cm (½ inch) piece fresh ginger
2 cloves garlic
2 tablespoons light soya sauce
1½ tablespoons hot bean paste, or *hoisin* sauce
1 tablespoon Chinese wine
2 teaspoons sugar
½ cup water
cornflour
2 teaspoons Chinese brown vinegar or lemon juice
1 teaspoon sesame oil
spring onion, chopped

Clean and scale fish and make several deep diagonal
cuts across each side. Heat 5 cm (2 inches) oil in a *wok*
and fry fish for 1 minute on each side. Lift out and keep
warm.

Chop ginger and garlic finely. Pour out all but 1
tablespoon oil. Fry ginger and garlic for 2 minutes, then
stir in soya sauce, bean paste or *hoisin* sauce, wine and
sugar. Cook for 1 minute, then add water and bring to
the boil. Return fish to the pan and simmer on moderate heat until fish is done. Turn once during cooking.

Carefully lift fish onto a serving dish. If necessary
thicken sauce with a little cornflour mixed with cold
water. Spoon sauce over the fish and sprinkle with
brown vinegar or lemon juice and sesame oil just before
serving. Garnish with chopped spring onion.

STUFFED CRAB CLAWS

12 crab pincers with meat intact
375 g (¾ lb) raw shrimp, peeled
100 g (3½ oz) fresh breadcrumbs
1 teaspoon salt
¼ teaspoon white pepper
3 teaspoons lemon juice
½ teaspoon dry mustard
2 egg whites
2 eggs, beaten
cornflour
white sesame seeds
oil for deep frying
12 small lettuce leaves
tomato slices

Break shell away from meat on pincers leaving meat
attached to the claw. (It will cling to the central sinew.)
Pound shrimp meat to a paste and add fresh
breadcrumbs, adding a little water if the mixture is too
dry. Season with salt, pepper, lemon juice and mustard
and bind with egg whites. Press mixture around the
crab meat to form a smooth ball with the claw tip
exposed. Coat very lightly with cornflour, then brush
with beaten egg. Dip the end of each ball into toasted
sesame seeds, coating thickly. Coat again with cornflour.

Heat oil and fry several claws at a time for about 2½
minutes until golden brown. Drain well. Place lettuce
on a serving plate and put a crab claw in the curl of each
leaf. Decorate the plate with sliced tomato.

LOBSTER WITH SALTED BLACK BEANS AND CHILLI

750 g (1½ lb) fresh lobster
3 teaspoons salted black beans
2 cloves garlic
1 teaspoon sugar
3 tablespoons oil
2 fresh red chillies, thinly sliced
1 cm (½ inch) piece fresh ginger, thinly sliced
¼ cup light chicken stock
1 tablespoon light soya sauce
pinch of white pepper
1 teaspoon ginger wine (see glossary)
1 teaspoon cornflour
1 spring onion, finely chopped

Cut lobster in half and discard inedible parts. Scoop
flesh from tail and scrape out shell. Drop head and
shell into a saucepan of boiling water and cook to a
bright red. Drain and brush gently to clean.

Cut lobster meat into bite-sized cubes. Crush black
beans with garlic and sugar and fry in oil for 2 minutes.
Add lobster and stir-fry until pink. Add chillies, ginger, chicken stock, soya sauce, pepper and ginger wine,
cover and simmer for 3 minutes. Mix cornflour with a
little cold water and stir into the sauce to thicken.
Spoon cooked lobster into the lobster shell and pour on
the sauce. Garnish with chopped spring onion.

SHRIMP WITH CASHEW NUTS AND VEGETABLES

250 g (½ lb) raw shrimp
salt
pepper
1½ tablespoons cornflour
75 g (2½ oz) celery, finely diced
60 g (2 oz) baby corn cobs, drained and cut into
   1 cm (½ inch) pieces
60 g (2 oz) cucumber, chopped (optional)
45 g (1½ oz) green pepper, chopped
75 g (2½ oz) button mushrooms or champignons,
   chopped
6 spring onions, finely chopped
60 g (2 oz) bamboo shoots, drained and chopped
oil
45 g (1½ oz) raw cashew nuts
1¾ cups chicken or fish stock
1 teaspoon salt
½ teaspoon white pepper
3 teaspoons dark soya sauce
1 tablespoon Chinese rice wine
fresh coriander leaves

Peel and devein shrimps and sprinkle with salt and
pepper. Coat lightly with cornflour.

Put all vegetables in a saucepan and pour in stock,
reserving 3 tablespoons. Bring to the boil and season
with salt and pepper. Cook for 2 minutes, then remove
from heat and drain.

Heat oil and gently deep fry cashews for 5 minutes.
Heat 2 tablespoons oil and stir-fry shrimp for 2 minutes. Add vegetables and a little more oil if necessary

and stir-fry for 2 minutes on high heat. Add salt, pepper, soya sauce and Chinese wine, stir, then pour in reserved stock. Thicken sauce with a little cornflour mixed with cold water and continue to cook until sauce clears.

Stir in fried cashew nuts. Spoon onto a warmed serving plate and garnish with fresh coriander leaves.

FRIED SHRIMP BALLS

375 g (¾ lb) raw shrimp, peeled
½ teaspoon salt
30 g (1 oz) pork fat, steamed
2 teaspoons Chinese rice wine
1 teaspoon sesame oil
2 egg whites
1 tablespoon cornflour
¼ teaspoon white pepper
oil for deep frying
sweet soya sauce or *hoisin* sauce

Smash shrimps with the side of a cleaver until reduced to a smooth pulp. Add salt and very finely diced pork fat. Work in remaining ingredients except for oil and sweet soya sauce and knead until smooth and well mixed.

Heat oil to smoking point. To make shrimp balls squeeze a ball of the paste from clenched fist out between thumb and forefinger. Scoop off with a spoon and drop into the oil. Deep fry until golden and crisp on the surface. Lift out and drain.

Serve with a dip of sweet soya sauce or *hoisin* sauce.

CRYSTAL PRAWNS

24 medium sized raw prawns
1 tablespoon ginger wine (see glossary)
1 tablespoon water
¼ teaspoon white pepper
4 spring onions
2.5 cm (1 inch) piece fresh ginger, sliced
1 carrot, sliced
oil

Peel away shells from prawns leaving heads and tails intact. With a small sharp knife cut a deep slit down the back of each prawn and scrape out the dark vein. Cut almost through the prawn. Marinate in ginger wine, water and pepper for 5 minutes.

Clean spring onions and cut into 8 cm (3 inch) pieces. Shred both ends of each piece and drop into a dish of iced water to curl. Cut decorative shapes from carrot and ginger slices using a vegetable cutter.

Heat about 3 tablespoons oil in a *wok* and stir-fry prawns until they turn pink and curl. Cook until flesh is just firm. Do not overcook. Lift onto a serving plate and decorate with spring onion curls, and sliced ginger and carrot. Serve with a bowl of dark soya sauce.

ABALONE IN OYSTER SAUCE

375 g (¾ lb) canned abalone
12 lettuce leaves
2 tablespoons oil

2 teaspoons sesame oil
⅓ cup chicken stock
2 teaspoons Chinese rice wine
1 tablespoon dark soya sauce
3 tablespoons oyster sauce
sugar
white pepper
cornflour

Drain abalone and cut into thin slices. Drop into a saucepan of boiling, slightly salted water and simmer for 2 minutes. Drain well. Drop lettuce into a pot of boiling water to which 1 tablespoon oil has been added. Remove at once and drain well. Arrange on a serving plate and sprinkle with sesame oil and remaining oil.

Bring remaining ingredients from chicken stock to oyster sauce to boil and season to taste with sugar and white pepper. Thicken with a little cornflour mixed with cold water if necessary. Put in abalone and simmer for 2 minutes, then spoon onto the lettuce and serve hot.

SCALLOPS WITH SHRIMP AND MUSHROOMS

12 large fresh scallops
220 g (7 oz) raw shrimp, peeled
2 teaspoons Chinese rice wine
2 teaspoons light soya sauce
6 dried Chinese mushrooms, soaked
6 canned or fresh straw mushrooms
1 cm (½ inch) piece fresh ginger, shredded
4 spring onions, shredded
1½ tablespoons oil
1 teaspoon sugar
salt
white pepper
⅔ cup light chicken or fish stock
1 heaped teaspoon cornflour
2 egg whites

Wash scallops in salted water and drain well. Cut shrimps open down the backs and scrape out dark veins. Wash well. Place scallops and shrimp in a dish and pour on wine and soya sauce. Marinate for 10 minutes.

Drain mushrooms and remove stems. Cut in halves. Lightly boil fresh straw mushrooms or drain canned mushrooms and rinse in cold water. Cut in halves.

Heat oil and fry ginger and spring onions for 1 minute. Add scallops and cook for 2 minutes, then add mushrooms and season with sugar, salt and pepper. Add shrimp and cook for another minute on moderate to low heat. Pour in stock and bring to the boil. Thicken with cornflour mixed with a little cold water. Stir in lightly beaten egg whites which will form white threads in the sauce. Do not stir again until egg sets. Transfer to a serving dish and serve at once.

SAUTEED EEL WITH BAMBOO SHOOTS AND MUSHROOMS

500 g (1 lb) fresh eel
30 g (1 oz) fat pork

Eggplant Szechwan Style, and Ma Po Beancurd (recipes page 74).

3 tablespoons oil
6 spring onions, sliced
4 cm (1½ inch) piece fresh ginger, thinly sliced
90 g (3 oz) canned bamboo shoots
8 dried Chinese mushrooms, soaked
1 tablespoon Chinese rice wine
2 tablespoons dark soya sauce
3 teaspoons sugar
¾ cup water, fish or chicken stock
3 teaspoons Chinese brown vinegar
3 teaspoons sesame oil
2 teaspoons cornflour
6 spring onion shoots or chive shoots

Clean and skin eel and drop into a pot of boiling water. Remove after 10 seconds. Wipe dry and cut into 2.5 cm (1 inch) pieces. Dice fat pork and saute in oil with onion and ginger. Drain and slice bamboo shoots and mushrooms thinly and add to the pan. Saute for 2 minutes, then season with wine, soya sauce and sugar. Add eel and water or stock and simmer until eel is tender.

Add vinegar and sesame oil and thicken sauce with cornflour mixed with a little cold water. Cook until sauce thickens and clears. Spoon onto a serving dish and garnish with chopped spring onion or chive shoots.

PEKING DUCK WITH PANCAKES

3 kg (6 lb) fat duck
¾ cup boiling water
1 cup golden syrup
3 star anise
1 heaped teaspoon Chinese five-spice powder

Pancakes:
185 g (6 oz) plain flour
½ cup boiling water
sesame oil

Garnishes:
spring onion curls
sweet bean paste or *hoisin* sauce

Clean and wash duck. Dry thoroughly inside and out. Dilute golden syrup in the boiling water then bring to the boil. Add crumbled star anise. Rub the bird inside and out with Chinese five-spice powder. Hold the duck oven a large bowl and pour the boiling syrup into the cavity and over the skin.

Tie a strong string around the neck and hang the duck over a drip tray in a draughty place to dry for 5 hours. If necessary, direct an electric fan onto the bird to hasten the drying. This process makes the skin crisp when cooked.

Brush the bird with remaining syrup solution and place on a rack in a baking tin. Roast in a preheated moderately hot oven for 1 hour. Turn and roast for a further ¾ hour or until cooked through. Test if done by inserting a skewer into the thickest part of the thigh. If no pink liquid escapes the bird is done. Peking Duck should not be overcooked.

To prepare pancakes, sieve flour into a mixing bowl and pour in water. Work with a wooden spoon until dough is completely amalgamated. Add a little more water if needed. When cool enough to handle transfer to a floured board and knead briskly for 10 minutes. Cover with a damp cloth and leave to stand in a warm place for 15 minutes. Roll on a floured board into a long sausage. Cut off walnut-sized pieces and press flat. Brush one side with sesame oil and stick two pieces together, oiled sides meeting. Roll out the two pancakes together until paper thin.

Heat a heavy frying pan or hot plate and cook pressed-together pancakes on moderate heat until brown flecks appear. Turn and cook other side, then peel apart. Do not cook the inside surfaces. Cook all pancakes in this way and keep wrapped in a cloth until ready to serve.

To prepare spring onion curls, cut off the lower white section and shred with a sharp knife at each end, discarding green tops. Drop into a bowl of very iced water to make them curl.

To serve Peking Duck, first slice off the skin, then the meat. Arrange on a serving plate. Serve pancakes and spring onions on another plate and pour sauce into small dipping dishes.

BEGGAR'S CHICKEN

2 kg (4 lb) chicken
12 dried Chinese mushrooms, soaked
155 g (5 oz) Tientsin preserved vegetables
100 g (3½ oz) fat pork
3 tablespoons oil
1 tablespoon dark soya sauce
2 teaspoons Chinese rice wine
2 teaspoons sugar
pinch of white pepper
4 lotus leaves (or use spinach or cabbage)
newspaper or plain paper
1½ kg (3 lb) clay or plain flour

Wash and wipe chicken. Drain and chop mushrooms and preserved vegetables. Dice pork finely. Saute pork in oil until cooked through. Add mushrooms, vegetables and all seasonings and stir-fry for 5 minutes. Cool slightly. Stuff the mixture into the cavity of the bird and secure the opening with toothpicks or sew up carefully.

Cover chicken with lotus leaves, or other leaves. Wrap in newspaper or plain paper and encase in the prepared clay. If using flour, make into a stiff dough with water and wrap the paste around the bird after first wrapping in paper. Ensure there are no cracks which will allow the juices to escape. Place on a baking sheet in a moderately hot oven for 1¾-2 hours. The bird should be so tender that the flesh falls from the bones.

Break open casing and tear away paper and leaves before serving.

PAPER-WRAPPED CHICKEN

375 g (¾ lb) chicken
3 teaspoons sesame oil
2 teaspoons salt
1 teaspoon Chinese five-spice powder
¼ teaspoon crushed star anise
heavy-duty cellophane or greaseproof paper
oil for deep frying

Cut chicken into small dice. Mix remaining ingredients and pour over the chicken. Mix well and leave to marinate for ½ hour. Cut cellophane into 20 cm (8 inch) squares. Divide meat between the paper sheets and fold up, tucking the last end in securely.

Heat oil to smoking point and carefully lower in the packages. Deep fry for 1½-2 minutes. Lift out and drain thoroughly before serving, still in paper wrapping. Each diner unwraps his chicken just before eating.

ONE-POT CHICKEN WITH RICE AND CHINESE SAUSAGE

375 g (¾ lb) short grain rice
3 cups light chicken stock
185 g (6 oz) chicken breast
3 dried Chinese mushrooms, soaked
1 dried Chinese sausage
2 spring onions, shredded
pinch of salt
white pepper
½ teaspoon sugar
1 tablespoon light soya sauce
1 teaspoon sesame oil
1 teaspoon cornflour
1 tablespoon water

Wash rice and put into a casserole with chicken stock. Bring to the boil, cover and reduce heat. Cook until beginning to soften and water reduced to the level of the rice. Cut chicken into 2.5 cm (1 inch) cubes and scatter over the rice. Drain and slice mushrooms, wash and slice sausage. Add to the pot with remaining ingredients. Cover and continue to cook until the rice is done and meat tender. Any liquid in the pot should be absorbed into the rice. Stir with chopsticks to distribute meat through the rice. Serve at once.

STIR-FRIED CHICKEN AND GREEN PEPPERS

375 g (¾ lb) chicken breast
1 egg white
1 tablespoon cornflour
1 tablespoon soya sauce
2 teaspoons ginger wine (see glossary)
2 teaspoons sesame oil
½ teaspoon salt
¼ teaspoon white pepper
2 green peppers
1 fresh red chilli
2 cloves garlic
2½ tablespoons oil
2 teaspoons white vinegar
1 teaspoon sugar
2 teaspoons Chinese rice wine
1 teaspoon sesame oil
2 tablespoons water
salt
cornflour

Skin chicken and cut into 2.5 cm (1 inch) cubes. Put into a basin and add egg white and cornflour. Mix with

a chopstick. Mix ingredients from soya sauce to white pepper and pour over the chicken. Stir well and leave to marinate for 15 minutes.

Cut peppers into 2.5 cm (1 inch) pieces, discarding seeds. Seed and slice chilli. Chop garlic finely. Heat oil and stir-fry peppers, chilli and garlic for 2 minutes. Remove and set aside. Add chicken and stir-fry until lightly coloured. Add remaining ingredients except cornflour and continue to stir on moderate to high heat until chicken is cooked through. Return peppers, chilli and garlic to the pan.

Mix a little cornflour with cold water and pour into the pan. Stir until the sauce thickens slightly and becomes clear. Check seasonings.

LEMON CHICKEN

1½ kg (3 lb) chicken
salt
white pepper
1½ teaspoons sugar
½ tablespoon Chinese rice wine
2 tablespoons custard powder
2 egg yolks
oil for deep frying

Sauce:
¼ cup lemon juice
¾ teaspoon white vinegar
½ cup light chicken stock
60 g (2 oz) sugar
3 teaspoons cornflour
3-4 drops yellow food colouring
lemon slices

Prepare chicken and pat dry. Mix salt and pepper with sugar and Chinese wine and rub into the chicken inside and out. Leave for 15 minutes. Place in a steamer and cook for 45 minutes. Leave to cool. Coat the bird with custard powder, then brush with beaten egg.

Heat oil and carefully lower in the bird. Deep fry until skin is golden brown and crisp. Lift out and drain well, then cut into serving pieces.

Put all sauce ingredients into a small saucepan and bring to the boil, stirring until it becomes clear. Check taste and add more sugar or lemon as preferred. Pour over the chicken and garnish with lemon slices.

BRAISED CHICKEN WINGS IN OYSTER SAUCE

12 chicken wings
1 tablespoon dark soya sauce
8 stalks Chinese cabbage or spring greens
oil for deep frying
½ teaspoon sesame oil
pinch of salt
pinch of white pepper
1½ tablespoons oyster sauce
1 teaspoon sugar
1 teaspoon sesame oil
½ cup water
2 teaspoons cornflour

Cut chicken wings in halves at the joint. Pour on dark

soya sauce and rub well into the skin to colour. Leave for 10 minutes, then deep fry until golden brown.

Cut vegetables into 8 cm (3 inch) sections and drop into a saucepan of boiling salted water. Cook until tender, then lift out and drain very well. Heat 3 tablespoons oil and stir-fry vegetables for 2 minutes. Season with sesame oil, salt and pepper and arrange on a serving dish. Keep warm.

Put chicken wings back into the pan, cover and simmer until cooked through. Add remaining ingredients except cornflour and simmer for 4 minutes. Mix cornflour with a little water and add to the pan. Stir until sauce thickens and begins to clear. Check seasoning. Arrange the chicken wings on the vegetables. Pour on sauce.

SAUTEED FROGS LEGS WITH SESAME AND CHILLI

375 g (¾ lb) frogs legs
3 teaspoons Chinese rice wine
2 teaspoons cornflour
3 tablespoons oil
1 fresh red chilli, thinly sliced
3 spring onions, shredded
1½ tablespoons light soya sauce
1 teaspoon sugar
½ teaspoon salt
pinch of white pepper
1 tablespoon sesame oil
fresh coriander leaves

Divide frogs legs at the central joint. Sprinkle with Chinese wine and cornflour. Leave for 10 minutes. Heat oil and stir-fry frogs legs until light gold in colour. Add sliced chilli and shredded onions and fry briefly, then add soya sauce and remaining seasonings and cook on lowered heat for 3 minutes.

Sprinkle on sesame oil and heat again briefly. Transfer to a serving dish and garnish with fresh coriander.

MEATBALLS ON SPINACH

Makes 24.

500 g (1 lb) beef steak
45 g (1½ oz) pork fat
2 spring onions
4 sprigs fresh coriander
½ teaspoon grated lemon rind
2 teaspoons salt
2 tablespoons dark soya sauce
pinch of white pepper
1½ teaspoons sesame oil
1 teaspoon bicarbonate of soda
3 tablespoons cornflour
3 tablespoons water
24 spinach leaves
2 tablespoons vegetable oil

Mince beef finely with pork fat, spring onions and coriander. Blend in lemon rind, salt, soya sauce, pepper, sesame oil and baking soda and work to a smooth paste.

Add cornflour and water and knead until smooth. Form into 24 balls. Leave for 15 minutes.

Wash spinach leaves and arrange on a fireproof plate. Sprinkle on half the oil and place meatballs on top. Sprinkle with remaining oil and place over a steamer to cook for about 12 minutes. Serve with hot mustard.

SZECHWAN BEEF STEW

AU LAM

1 kg (2 lb) stewing beef, preferably shin or flank
3 whole star anise
1 large onion, sliced
2.5 cm (1 inch) piece fresh ginger, sliced
1 dried tangerine peel or 1 lemon rind
2 tablespoons oil
6 cloves garlic
2 teaspoons black peppercorns, crushed
2 teaspoons Chinese brown peppercorns
¾ cup dark soya sauce
¼ cup Chinese rice wine
3 tablespoons sweet bean paste or *hoisin* sauce

Cut meat into 5 cm (2 inch) cubes. Place in a deep pot and cover with water. Add star anise, onion, ginger and tangerine peel or lemon rind. Cover and bring to the boil, then reduce heat and simmer for at least 2 hours.

Heat oil in a small saucepan and add chopped garlic and peppercorns. Fry for 1 minute, then add soya sauce, wine and bean paste or *hoisin* sauce. Bring to the boil and remove from the heat. Skim off any froth and pour the sauce into the meat. Cover and cook for a further 1 hour. Remove star anise and peel before serving.

SHREDDED BEEF COUNTRY STYLE

250 g (½ lb) frying steak
3 tablespoons dark soya sauce
1 tablespoon Chinese rice wine
2 teaspoons sugar
1 teaspoon ginger juice
1 tablespoon cornflour
2 egg whites
125 g (¼ lb) celery
125 g (¼ lb) green beans
1 small carrot
1 small onion
2-3 fresh red chillies
oil for deep frying
2 teaspoons sesame oil
white pepper

Slice beef across the grain, then cut into fine shreds. Mix ingredients from soya sauce to egg whites and pour over the meat. Stir well and leave for 10 minutes to marinate.

Cut celery and green beans into matchstick pieces. Scrape carrot and cut into strips. Slice onion and chillies thinly.

Heat about 10 cm (4 inches) oil in a pan. Place shredded meat in a wire frying basket and lower into the hot oil. Fry until dark and crisp. Lift out and drain well. Pour off most of the oil. Put in vegetables and fry until

Steamed Whole Fish with Ginger and Green Onion, and Sweet and Sour Fish Fingers (recipes page 64).

cooked but still crisp. Put with the meat, mix well and sprinkle on sesame oil and white pepper.

SHREDDED PORK WITH VERMICELLI IN SESAME BUNS

125 g (¼ lb) lean pork
90 g (3 oz) transparent vermicelli
3 tablespoons oil
1 cm (½ inch) piece fresh ginger, finely shredded
3 spring onions, finely shredded
3 teaspoons hot bean paste
1 teaspoon salt
2 tablespoons dark soya sauce
1 teaspoon sugar
1 cup beef stock
2 teaspoons cornflour
2 teaspoons sesame oil

Slice pork thinly, then cut into thin shreds. Soak vermicelli in warm water to soften. Drain and cut into 2.5 cm (1 inch) pieces. Heat oil and fry pork until well coloured. Add ginger and spring onions and fry for 2 minutes, then add bean paste and stir on moderate heat for 1 minute. Add vermicelli and salt, soya sauce, sugar and stock. Bring to the boil and simmer until pork and vermicelli are tender and liquid almost absorbed.

Mix cornflour with a very little cold water and stir into the meat. Leave to thicken slightly, then sprinkle on sesame oil. Serve with crispy sesame buns. Cut the buns in halves and stuff with the pork and vermicelli mixture.

Sesame Buns:
1 cup plain flour
¾ cup vegetable oil
750 g (1½ lb) plain flour
1½ cups boiling water
cold water
1½ teaspoons salt
30 g (1 oz) white sesame seeds

Pour 1 cup plain flour and vegetable oil into a pan and fry on moderate heat, stirring, until the flour is coloured a rich golden brown and is very fragrant. Leave the flour oil to cool.

Sieve remaining 750 g (1½ lb) flour into a mixing bowl and add boiling water. Work with chopsticks until incorporated, then add cold water and salt to make a smooth, fairly stiff dough. Knead for 10 minutes on a lightly floured board. Cover with a damp cloth and leave for 15 minutes, then knead for a further 5 minutes. Roll out to about 2 mm (1/16 inch) thick. Spread the flour oil thickly over the dough and roll up into a long tube. Cut into 2.5 cm (1 inch) lengths.

Roll each piece out across the folds, fold two ends in and turn the dough to one side. Roll out again, working away from the body. Continue rolling, folding and rolling for about five times. Press sesame seeds onto each piece and roll out into a 13 cm (5 inch) long cake, about 4 cm (1½ inches) wide. Place on a floured baking sheet and bake in a preheated hot oven for 7 minutes, turn and cook the other side for about 3 minutes. Cool slightly before cutting in halves.

TWICE-COOKED PORK

250 g (½ lb) pork belly with skin
1 green pepper
8 chive shoots
6 cloves garlic
4 tablespoons oil
2 teaspoons Chinese rice wine
1 tablespoon hot bean paste
1 tablespoon sweet bean paste
1½ tablespoons dark soya sauce
2 tablespoons chicken stock or water
1 teaspoon sugar
¼ teaspoon white pepper
1 teaspoon cornflour
1 teaspoon sesame oil
white pepper

Place pork piece in a saucepan and cover with water. Bring to the boil then reduce heat and simmer for 45 minutes. Lift out and drain well. Slice very thinly. Cut pepper into 2.5 cm (1 inch) squares. Cut chive shoots into 5 cm (2 inch) pieces and slice garlic.

Heat oil and fry sliced pork over high heat for 3 minutes. Add chive shoots and garlic and fry for another 2 minutes. Add bean pastes, Chinese wine, soya sauce and pepper squares and simmer, stirring continually, for 3 minutes. Add stock or water with sugar and white pepper. Boil for about 5 minutes until pork is tender.

Thicken with cornflour mixed with a little cold water and stir until sauce clears. Sprinkle with sesame oil and season with white pepper before serving.

BARBECUED SPARE RIBS

1¼ kg (2½ lb) pork spare ribs
3 tablespoons dark soya sauce
1 tablespoon sweet bean paste
2 tablespoons sugar
3 cloves garlic
1 tablespoon Chinese rice wine
¼ teaspoon Chinese five-spice powder

Separate ribs and trim each neatly at the ends. Mix remaining ingredients together and pour over the ribs. Allow to marinate for 2 hours.

Place ribs on a rack and cook under a moderate grill until cooked through and crispy on the surface, or cook over a charcoal barbecue. Brush with the marinating liquid during cooking to keep meat moist.

STEWED SPARE RIBS WITH SALTED BLACK BEANS

375 g (¾ lb) pork spare ribs
2 tablespoons salted black beans
4 cloves garlic
3 spring onions
1 cm (½ inch) piece fresh ginger
1 fresh red chilli
3 tablespoons oil
1 teaspoon sugar
2 tablespoons dark soya sauce

2 tablespoons water
1 tablespoon Chinese rice wine
2 teaspoons sesame oil

Separate ribs and cut into 2.5 cm (1 inch) pieces. Crush black beans with garlic. Finely chop spring onions, ginger and chilli. Heat oil and fry spare ribs until well coloured. Add crushed bean paste and fry for an additional minute, then add onion, ginger and chilli and stir on moderate heat for 1 minute.

Pour in sugar, soya sauce, water and Chinese wine. Cover pan and turn heat down very low. Stew for about 45 minutes until ribs are very tender. Check seasonings and sprinkle on sesame oil.

THICK AND THIN NOODLES IN SOUP

250 g (½ lb) *hor fun* rice flour noodles
250 g (½ lb) thin rice vermicelli
90 g (3 oz) pigs liver
90 g (3 oz) lean pork
60 g (2 oz) raw peeled shrimp
90 g (3 oz) green beans (optional)
125 g (¼ lb) green vegetables such as spinach, cabbage, lettuce
3 tablespoons oil
2 cloves garlic, crushed
¼ cup light soya sauce
sugar
white pepper
6 cups chicken or beef stock
2 teaspoons cornflour

Put *hor fun* noodles in a basin and cover with boiling water. Cover thin rice noodles with cold water. Leave to soften. Slice liver thinly and remove any membrane. Finely shred pork. Chop shrimps, beans and vegetables.

Heat oil and fry garlic for 1 minute. Add drained *hor fun* noodles and fry for 2 minutes. Transfer to a serving bowl. Add liver and pork to the pan and fry for 5 minutes, adding a little more oil if needed. Add shrimp, beans and remaining seasonings. Pour on stock and bring to the boil. Add vegetables and simmer for 3 minutes, then thicken soup slightly with cornflour mixed with a little cold water. Finally, drop in thin rice vermicelli. Heat through and pour over the *hor fun* noodles.

FRIED EGG NOODLES WITH BEEF AND GREEN VEGETABLES

125 g (¼ lb) frying steak
1 tablespoon dark soya sauce
2 teaspoons Chinese rice wine
2 teaspoons cornflour
1 teaspoon sesame oil
pinch of sugar
pinch of white pepper
185 g (6 oz) thin egg noodles
3 tablespoons oil
100 g (3½ oz) green vegetables such as snow peas, celery, green pepper, beans, cabbage

3 spring onions
1 cm (½ inch) piece fresh ginger
½ cup beef stock
1 teaspoon cornflour
2 teaspoons dark soya sauce
½ teaspoon sugar

Slice beef thinly, then cut into strips and marinate in a mixture of dark soya sauce, Chinese wine, cornflour, sesame oil, sugar and white pepper. Leave for 15 minutes.

Drop egg noodles into boiling water to soften. Drain well. Heat 2-3 teaspoons oil in a *wok* and fry noodles until dark and crisp on the edges. Turn over in one piece and fry other side. Do not cook noodles with too much oil or they will become very greasy. Lift onto a serving plate and keep warm.

Drop vegetables into boiling water and leave to soften. Hard vegetables can be boiled briefly. Drain and add to the pan with remaining oil, spring onions cut into 2.5 cm (1 inch) lengths and shredded ginger. Stir-fry for 2 minutes, then pour over noodles.

Fry marinated beef for 2-3 minutes, then add beef stock mixed with cornflour and dark soya sauce. Sprinkle on sugar and simmer until sauce thickens. Spoon over noodles and serve at once.

CRISPY RICE VERMICELLI WITH CHICKEN AND VEGETABLES

185 g (6 oz) rice vermicelli
90 g (3 oz) chicken breast
30 g (1 oz) chicken livers
6 dried Chinese mushrooms, soaked
60 g (2 oz) canned bamboo shoots
90 g (3 oz) *bok choy* cabbage
2 teaspoons Chinese rice wine
1 tablespoon light soya sauce
white pepper
2 teaspoons cornflour
3 tablespoons oil
¾ cup chicken stock
1 teaspoon sesame oil
salt
white pepper
2 spring onions, shredded
oil for deep frying

Break vermicelli into 5 cm (2 inch) pieces. Slice chicken thinly and chop livers. Drain and slice mushrooms and bamboo shoots and cut *bok choy* into 5 cm (2 inch) pieces. Heat a saucepan of water until boiling and put in *bok choy*. Cook until tender, then drain.

Marinate chicken in a mixture of rice wine, soya sauce, white pepper and cornflour for 5 minutes. Heat oil and fry chicken until lightly coloured. Add livers and cook until no pink shows, then add mushroms and bamboo shoots, *bok choy* and chicken stock. Boil for 1 minute, then season with sesame oil, salt and pepper. Thicken sauce slightly with a little cornflour mixed with cold water if necessary. Add spring onions.

Heat 5 cm (2 inches) oil in a deep pan and when very hot put in noodles. They will immediately expand and become very crisp. Cook for about 30 seconds. Lift out and drain. Place on a serving plate and pour on the chicken and vegetables.

FRIED CANTONESE RICE

750 g (1½ lb) cooked white rice
3 tablespoons lard
2 eggs
60 g (2 oz) raw peeled shrimp
60 g (2 oz) roast pork
1 large onion
4 spring onions
60 g (2 oz) frozen green peas
4 dried Chinese mushrooms, soaked
1 tablespoon dark soya sauce
1 teaspoon sugar
white pepper
salt
1 teaspoon sesame oil
finely chopped fresh coriander leaves

Fry rice in lard until grains are well coated. Set aside. Beat eggs and drop into the pan. Swirl pan so egg forms a very thin pancake. Cook until firm, then lift out. Allow to cool then shred finely.

Put in shrimps and cook until pink, then remove from pan and spoon over the rice. Cook pork for 1 minute adding more lard if needed. Add finely chopped onion and spring onions and cook for another minute. Put in peas and thinly sliced mushroom and stir-fry for a further 2 minutes. Splash in soya sauce and add sugar. Stir, then return rice and shrimps to pan. Season with white pepper and salt, if needed, and stir on moderate heat until warmed through.

Transfer to a serving dish. Sprinkle an oil. Decorate with finely shredded egg and fresh coriander.

MA PO BEANCURD

½ cup oil
6 squares soft beancurd
90 g (3 oz) minced beef
90 g (3 oz) minced pork
8 cloves garlic, finely chopped
4 spring onions, finely chopped
1½ tablespoons hot bean paste
¼ teaspoon white pepper, or
    1½ teaspoons chilli oil
3 tablespoons dark soya sauce
½ cup beef stock
2 teaspoons cornflour
pinch of monosodium glutamate
1½ teaspoons sesame oil

Choose well-drained firm pieces of beancurd. Heat oil in a frying pan. Drain beancurd and hold in the palm of the hand. Carefully cut into cubes, then transfer to a slice and lower into the pan. Fry the beancurd without stirring to avoid breaking the cubes. Cook to a light golden brown. Lift out and set aside.

Add minced beef and pork to the pan and fry to a light brown before adding garlic, onion, bean paste, pepper or chilli oil and soya sauce. Cook for 3 minutes, then add beef stock mixed with cornflour, and monosodium glutamate. Bring to the boil, reduce heat and simmer until sauce is thickened and meat is well seasoned. Return beancurd and cook for 2 minutes. Transfer to a serving dish and splash with sesame oil.

EGGPLANT SZECHWAN STYLE

375 g (¾ lb) eggplants
4 tablespoons oil
2 teaspoons sesame oil
6 spring onions
8 cloves garlic
1 cm (½ inch) piece fresh ginger
2 tablespoons *hoisin* sauce
1½ teaspoons sugar
2 tablespoons dark soya sauce
1½ teaspoons Chinese brown vinegar
⅓ cup chicken or beef stock
2 teaspoons cornflour
2 teaspoons sesame oil

Wipe eggplants, remove stalks but do not peel. Cut into 2.5 cm (1 inch) thick slices. Heat oil, add sesame oil and fry both sides of sliced eggplant for 1 minute. Turn heat down and cook until soft, then remove from pan and drain on absorbent paper.

Chop spring onions, garlic and ginger finely. Add to the pan with a little more oil if needed and fry for 1 minute. Add remaining ingredients except cornflour and sesame oil and bring to the boil. Simmer for 3 minutes, then return eggplant and cook for 10 minutes on moderate to low heat. Thicken sauce with cornflour mixed with a little cold water and cook until clear. Sprinkle on sesame oil.

Thinly sliced red chilli can be added at the same time as the spring onions to make this dish more piquant.

SAUTE OF GREEN VEGETABLES WITH CRABMEAT DRESSING

500 g (1 lb) Chinese cabbage or Chinese long leaf
    lettuce
4 cups water
2 tablespoons oil
½ teaspoon salt
90 g (3 oz) cooked or canned crabmeat
2 teaspoons cornflour
⅓ cup water
2 egg whites
salt
white pepper
1 teaspoon light soya sauce
½ teaspoon sesame oil
3 teaspoons crab roe, crumbled (optional)

Wash cabbage or lettuce and shake out water. Break leaves from stem, discarding centre core. Bring water to boil with 1 tablespoon oil and when bubbling put in cabbage or lettuce. Reduce heat slightly and cook cabbage for 30-40 seconds, lettuce for a maximum of 20 seconds. Lift out and drain well. Arrange vegetables on a serving dish and splash with remaining oil.

Flake crabmeat and put into a small saucepan with cornflour mixed with water. Bring to the boil and stir until slightly thickened. When sauce is just bubbling slowly, pour in beaten egg white so it forms white threads in the sauce. Do not stir until the egg sets. Season with salt, white pepper and soya sauce. Pour dressing over the vegetable and sprinkle on sesame oil and crab roe.

Toffee Apples (recipe page 77).

MIXED GREEN VEGETABLES WITH SALTED BLACK BEANS

500 g (1 lb) mixed green vegetables
2 cloves garlic
1 tablespoon salted black beans
1½ teaspoons sugar
3 tablespoons oil
6 spring onions, coarsely chopped
white pepper
1 teaspoon sesame oil

Choose vegetables such as long or green beans, snow peas, Chinese cabbage, kale, *bok choy*. Wash and slice vegetables. String snow peas and leave whole. Crush garlic and mash with salted beans and sugar.

Heat oil in a *wok* and fry the crushed beans for 1 minute. Put in harder green vegetables with spring onions and cook until beginning to soften, then add softer vegetables. Cover pan and allow vegetables to cook in their own steam for about 4 minutes on moderate to low heat. Splash in a very little water if the pan begins to dry. Season with white pepper and sesame oil. Serve at once.

SPRING ROLLS

Makes 24.

Wrappers:
220 g (7 oz) plain flour
3 eggs
1 teaspoon salt

Sift flour and salt into a mixing bowl and make well in the centre. Break in eggs and stir until the mixture begins to amalgamate. Remove to a floured board and knead gently. When all flour is worked in, knead strongly for several minutes. The more the dough is worked, the more elastic it will be, thereby making the pastry thinner and flakier. Roll out into a long loaf and cut into several pieces to make rolling out easier. While one piece is being rolled, cover remaining pieces with a damp cloth.

Dust a board with flour and with a floured rolling pin press down as hard as possible during rolling to make the pastry paper thin and transparent enough to see the board through. Take care not to break the pastry. Cut into 15 cm (6 inch) squares, cover with a damp cloth and prepare remaining dough. Cut each square into 2 triangular-shaped pieces.

Frozen wrappers may be used for convenience.

Filling:
100 g (3½ oz) minced pork, lightly fried
8 dried Chinese mushrooms, soaked
6 canned water chestnuts, chopped
1 tablespoon finely chopped fresh coriander leaves
4 spring onions, minced
30 g (1 oz) canned bamboo shoot, finely chopped
1 small carrot, grated
45 g (1½ oz) beanshoots
45 g (1½ oz) raw shrimps
1 teaspoon sugar
1½ tablespoons dark soya sauce
1 clove garlic, crushed (optional)

3 teaspoons cornflour
2 teaspoons salt
2 tablespoons oil

Drain mushrooms, remove stems and shred finely. Shred spring onion. Wash beanshoots and steep in boiling water for 2 minutes. Drain and cool. Peel shrimps and rinse. Mix all ingredients except oil in a large bowl. Heat oil and saute filling for 2-3 minutes. Allow to cool completely.

To fill spring rolls, place a heaped tablespoon of the filling on the wrapper. Turn in two ends, fold over and stick last end down with a little water. If using frozen wrappers start down one corner, fold over the filling, fold in two sides, then stick the last flap down with water.

Heat oil for deep frying and fry spring rolls, several at a time, until golden brown. Drain on absorbent paper. Return to the oil briefly before serving to crisp. Serve with soya sauce.

SEASONED BAMBOO SHOOTS

500 g (1 lb) canned young bamboo shoots
oil for deep frying
2 tablespoons sweet bean paste
2 tablespoons dark soya sauce
1 tablespoon sugar
3 teaspoons Chinese rice wine
2 tablespoons water
pinch of white pepper
250 g (½ lb) leaf spinach
2 teaspoons sesame oil

Drain bamboo shoots and cut into 2 cm (¾ inch) cubes. Place in a large perforated ladle or strainer and lower into hot oil to fry until well coloured. Lift out and drain.

Place bamboo shoots in a dry pan with bean paste, soya sauce, sugar and rice wine. Add 2 tablespoons oil from the other pan and bring sauce to the boil. Add water and simmer until sauce is well reduced and bamboo shoots tender. Season with white pepper.

Drop spinach into boiling water to soften. Drain. Stir-fry in 1 tablespoon oil for 2 minutes, then arrange on a serving dish. Place seasoned bamboo shoots on top and sprinkle with sesame oil.

SPICY PORK BUNS

Dough:
750 g (1½ lb) plain flour
125 g (¼ lb) sugar
1 tablespoon baking powder
2 tablespoons melted lard
¾ cup water

Filling:
500 g (1 oz) Chinese roast pork
1 cup water
1 teaspoon cornflour
3 teaspoons potato flour (or extra cornflour)
3 teaspoons dark soya sauce
1 tablespoon oyster sauce
pinch of salt
1½ tablespoons sugar

2 cloves garlic, minced
2 spring onions, minced
30 g (1 oz) pork fat, diced
2 tablespoons oil

Sieve flour into a basin and add sugar and baking powder. Make a well in the centre and pour in melted lard. Mix lightly into the flour, then add water and work to a smooth dough. Knead for 8 minutes, then cover with a damp cloth and leave to rise for 30 minutes.

Slice roast pork then cut into small pieces. Put into a saucepan with all filling ingredients except spring onions, pork fat and oil and simmer on low heat for 10 minutes.

Steam pork fat for 10 minutes, and add to the roast pork mixture with spring onions. Fry the mixture in oil on moderate heat for 2 minutes.

Roll the dough out into a long sausage and cut off pieces about 5 cm (2 inches) long. Flatten with the fingers and fill with a spoonful of the mixture. Pull the dough up around the filling and twist the joins to seal well. Put a piece of plain paper on the joined part of each bun and place paper-side down in a steamer. Cover and leave to rise for a further 10 minutes, then steam over high heat for 20-25 minutes. Serve hot in the steaming baskets.

ASSORTED MEAT PLATTER

8 thin slices braised beef steak
8 thin slices Chinese roast pork
8 thin slices pressed boiled pork or sausage
90 g (3 oz) boiled chicken, shredded
90 g (3 oz) braised chicken livers, thinly sliced
90 g (3 oz) jelly fish or vermicelli sheets, soaked and
    shredded
10 spears canned asparagus
salt and pepper powder
sweet bean paste or plum sauce

Arrange the meat and liver in a pattern around a serving dish. Place two spears of asparagus between each different lot of meat. Sprinkle shredded jelly fish or vermicelli with sesame oil and pile into the centre.

Serve with dips of salt and pepper powder and sweet bean paste or plum sauce.

PEPPER AND SALT POWDER

4 tablespoons table salt
1 teaspoon finely ground black peppercorns

Roast salt in a dry pan on moderate heat until lightly coloured. Stir in pepper and heat through briefly. Store in a sealed jar.

TOFFEE APPLES

2 medium sized eating apples
100 g (3½ oz) plain flour
1 egg
1⅓-1½ cups water
250 g (½ lb) sugar
1 tablespoon oil
2 tablespoons white sesame seeds

flavourless vegetable oil for deep frying
iced water
ice cubes

Oil a serving plate lightly and have all ingredients and utensils on hand as this dish requires precision timing.

Peel apples, remove cores and cut each into 8 pieces. Lightly beat egg and combine with ⅓ - ½ cup water and flour to make a smooth, fairly thick batter. Put oil for deep·frying on to heat.

Mix sugar with 1 cup water and 1 tablespoon oil and bring to the boil. Simmer until it forms a thick, light coloured toffee. Test if toffee is ready by dropping a spoonful into iced water. If it hardens immediately the toffee is done. Add sesame seeds to the toffee and set near the cooker.

When oil is almost at smoking point coat several pieces of apple with the batter and put into the oil. Fry to a golden brown. Lift out with wooden chopsticks and place in the toffee syrup. When coated transfer to the iced water to harden. Place on the oiled serving plate. Cook all apple in this way and serve immediately with the bowl of ice water. Dip into the water again to harden if the toffee has begun to soften.

Firm ripe banana may be used in this way also, either sliced or whole.

SWEET PEANUT SOUP

185 g (6 oz) raw peanuts
2 tablespoons white sesame seeds
8 cups water
125 g (¼ lb) white sugar
4 tablespoons cornflour
½ cup thick cream

Place peanuts in a hot oven or under a moderate grill to roast until lightly coloured. Place in a cloth and rub off skins. Toast sesame seeds lightly and grind peanuts and sesame seeds to a fine powder in a heavy-duty blender, adding a little water if needed.

Pour into a saucepan with water and sugar and simmer until smooth and creamy. Strain to remove any large pieces of peanut and bring to the boil again. Mix cornflour with thick cream and stir into the soup. Heat through until thickened. Serve warm.

ALMOND JELLY WITH MIXED FRUITS

1 tablespoon gelatine
1½ cups lukewarm water
1 teaspoon almond extract, or to taste
45 g (1½ oz) sugar
¾ cup evaporated milk
canned fruit cocktail in syrup

Soften gelatine in lukewarm water and heat until dissolved. Mix in almond extract, sugar and evaporated milk and heat through, stirring to dissolve the sugar. Pour into a greased tray and leave to set.

When firm cut into diamond shaped pieces. Serve in glass dessert dishes topped with mixed fruit. Pour on a generous amount of the syrup. Serve chilled.

GLOSSARY

BEAN PASTE, SALTED: A brown paste of soya beans, also known as yellow bean paste.

BEAN PASTE, SWEET: Either a thick flavourful black paste made from fermented flour and spices; or a similar sweet paste made from soya beans.

BEANSHOOTS (BEANSPROUTS): Young shoots of mung beans. Can be bought fresh or tinned; if tinned, rinse in cold water before use.

CANDLENUTS: Waxy nut similar to macadamia, which can be used as a substitute.

CHAT MASALA: Blend of Indian spices (recipe page 24).

CHILLIES: Members of the Capsicum family, sometimes known as hot peppers, chillies can be used fresh, flaked or powdered. Fresh chillies are green (unripe) or red (ripe). The seeds, which are the hottest part, can be removed before use.

CHINESE RICE WINE: Pale dry sherry is a good substitute.

COCONUT MILK: Made by mixing the grated flesh of coconut with water. Can be bought as compressed cakes and dissolved in warm water to the required thickness, or made from desiccated coconut as follows: for every 250 g desiccated coconut, add 1 cup water and blend thoroughly; pour through muslin and squeeze hard to extract as much thick milk as possible. Add another 2 cups water and repeat process to obtain thin coconut milk.

CORIANDER: Seeds, leaves and roots are used extensively in Asian cooking. Fresh coriander is sometimes available; it can be grown at home from the dried spice seeds.

CURRY LEAVES: Sometimes available dried, they add a distinctive flavour to Indian and Malaysian dishes.

DASHI: Japanese stock, available packaged (recipe page 55).

DRIED PRAWNS OR SHRIMPS: Should be soaked in warm water before use.

DRIED SHRIMP PASTE: Pungent seasoning paste used throughout Southeast Asia.

FISH SAUCE: Thin salty sauce available at Chinese provision shops.

FLOUR: The many kinds of flour used in Asia are made from a variety of grains, pulses and tubers.

   Atta: Fine wholewheat flour, used in Indian breads.

   Besan: A fine yellow flour made from chickpeas.

   Cornflour: Finely ground maize flour used as a thickener in Chinese cooking. Arrowroot can be substituted, but *not* wheat flour.

   Gram: A general term for flours made from lentils, including chickpeas.

   Green pea: Made from mung beans. Often light green in colour, but sometimes white or pink, it is used for sweets in Malaysia and Indonesia. Arrowroot is a suitable substitute.

   Maida: Finely ground white wheat flour. Substitute all-purpose or plain flour.

   Potato: Often added to batters to give more elasticity.

   Rice: Made from finely ground white rice and used in sweets and some batters.

   Rice, glutinous: Becomes almost clear and sticky when cooked, and is used in sweets and batters. Has more elasticity than ordinary rice flour.

GARAM MASALA: Blend of Indian spices (recipe page 24).

GHEE: Clarified butter, available in tins.

GINGER JUICE: Made by grating and squeezing fresh ginger root.

GINGER WINE: Made by soaking shredded fresh ginger in Chinese wine or dry sherry for at least 24 hours. Will keep indefinitely in refrigerator.

KRUPUK: Small crisp wafers, usually made from prawns. Fry in hot oil for a few seconds.

LEMON GRASS: Sometimes known as citronella grass. The white bulbous portion is used for its lemony fragrance. Can be bought dried in strips, chopped or powdered. Substitute lemon peel.

LENGKUAS: Greater Galangal, a member of the Ginger family. Dried or powdered *lengkuas* is sometimes sold under the name *laos*.

MIRIN: Sweet *sake* used in Japanese cooking. Substitute sweet sherry.

MISO: Thick paste made from fermented soya beans.

MONOSODIUM GLUTAMATE: Crystals or powder used as a tenderiser to highlight flavours.

MUSTARD SEEDS: Small brownish-black seeds used as a pungent spice in Indian cooking.

OYSTER SAUCE: Adds a delicate fishy flavour to Chinese dishes.

PALM SUGAR: Compressed cakes of rich brown sugar from the aren palm or, less commonly, the coconut palm. Substitute dark-brown sugar.

SAKE: Japanese rice wine. Substitute light dry sherry.

SHALLOTS: Small purple onions that grow in clusters similar to garlic heads, they are used extensively in Asian cooking.

SOYA SAUCE: Available in three types: 'light', 'dark' and 'sweet'. Flavours differ, so be sure to use the type specified.

SPRING ONIONS: Tall dark-green leafy onions, of which the small white bulb section is the part most often used. Common in all Asian cooking.

STAR ANISE: Eight-pointed spice with rich aniseed flavour.

TAMARIND: Dried flesh of sour fruit, mixed with water to make acidulating liquid. Substitute vinegar or lemon juice mixed with a little water.

WASABI: Powdered green horseradish used in Japanese cooking and as a highly pungent garnish. Available in small cans. Substitute hot mustard powder or fresh, grated horseradish.

INDEX